CASCADE –

creativity across science, art, dyslexia, education

Editors – Morag Kiziewicz and Iain Biggs

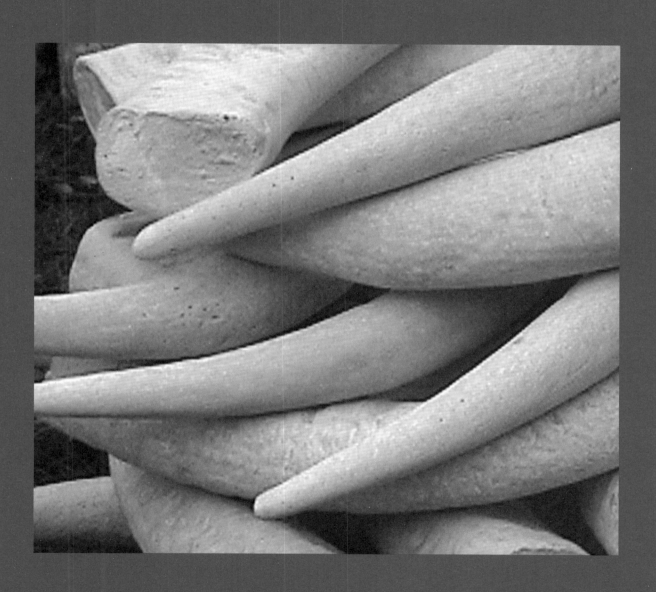

CONTENTS :
Cascade – creativity across science, art, dyslexia, education

FOREWORD

Professor Margaret Herrington

It is an honour to be asked to write a foreword to this collection of papers. Not having attended the conference, I experienced the set of papers entirely through their written (and visual) forms and so from the same vantage point as many future readers. However, though writing from the outside of the conference, I am not 'outside' many of the ideas discussed here and welcome the revisiting, re-questioning and re-tuning, as well as the new learning, which the collection offers.

For me, the collection represents a kind of intellectual, affective and sensory 'space' in, and through, which many voices are heard...some colliding...some bouncing off others...some agreeing...some in contest. It is a 'conversational' space in which dyslexic and non dyslexic listen and speak, bringing their own experiences and those of other thinkers and writers to the table, in a profoundly dialogic fashion. It is a conversation in which the unexpected jostles with the familiar, 'messiness' with clarity, and dazzling 'glimmers' of insight with 'solid' positions. This kind of 'open' space is rare in a field dominated by disciplinary boundaries and conventions.

The unifying themes within this dynamic are those of power and resistance. Who has the power to say that dyslexia exists or what dyslexia is/involves? Whose narratives are most highly valued? Who decides on methods of identification? Who determines how HE curriculum process, content and assessment will respond to dyslexia? Who decides on the nature of individual 'support'? Who exercises the power to exclude these kinds of discussions from HE? Many of the answers to these questions have been created largely by non dyslexic people. They are now embedded in everyday practices and sometimes oppressive conventions, and are resisted in many of the pieces here. Participants also resist aspects of each other's answers. As a reader I found myself resisting some of the narratives and claims here. This reflects the current 'reality' of multiple narratives about dyslexia competing for 'authenticity'.

The value of having differing narratives from dyslexic writers themselves cannot be over-emphasised. The descriptions of cognitive and sensory processing provide key 'insider' qualitative evidence for the field and should be recognised and scrutinised as such. Non dyslexic teachers and researchers, who do recognise this, are well represented here.

The resistance is also evident within the more general intellectual explorations by dyslexic writers. At every turn the writers challenge existing paradigms and raise profound questions; within and across disciplines. Though usefully focused on shared intellectual processes across disciplines, the writers also problematise those very processes; many concepts of creativity, for example, are developed and critiqued here. This work thus makes an important contribution to current explorations about discipline specific responses to dyslexia in HE

The closing speaker at the conference-Professor Jack Whitehead- asked that the 'life affirming energy' within the conference be celebrated. I found this reference to energy important because it is so frequently sapped by oppressive practices. As a reader I feel that this collection of papers allows me to feel, enjoy and celebrate some of that energy.

INTRODUCTION

In 2001 a conference called 'Cascade – creativity across science, art, dyslexia, education' was held at the University of Bath. The aim of the conference was to disseminate the outcomes of the Dyslexia strand of the WEBB accessibility project which had been a three year collaborative project funded by the Higher Education Funding Council for England (HEFCE) under the first strand of disability funding that was aimed at developing access for students with disabilities to Higher Education. The three Universities participating were the Universities of the West of England, Bristol and Bath. The collaborative project disseminated and explored through the event was called the 3 I's of Dyslexia: Identification, Intervention and Institutional issues, and one of the papers collected here is a comparative study of identification assessment methods for dyslexia by Dr Mary Haslum that resulted from the Project.

This three day event aimed to be fully accessible for dyslexia and therefore not all the presentations were in text. There were performance and music events, experiential workshops and an exhibition of painting, sculpture and ceramics. This book cannot fully do justice to the whole sense of the event, however the chapters by Ketaki Kushari Dyson and Andrew Henon aim to represent the exhibition and performance aspects, and some of the papers are accompanied by some examples of the visual art.

Much of the material from the conference was published on the cascade website (www.bath.ac.uk/cascade) but there was insufficient funding at the time to do justice to publishing the papers. It is unusual to find that there is a value in formally publishing these papers six years on, as conference events are traditionally rapidly superceded within research communities. There have been two further strands of HEFCE disability funding since this project completed, the last projects have recently completed and disseminated their work. Disability is now included within Widening Participation and Teaching and Learning agendas in Universities, there has been active representation of disability related issues and the new Disability Discrimination Bill requires the development of Disability Equality Schemes by all public institutions.

It would seem then that all the work towards inclusion for dyslexia is all done and these papers could represent a historical perspective into the exclusion of dyslexia in the past. Unfortunately this is not the case. One of the things that made this conference different was that this conference included dyslexic people speaking for themselves. Further, they were dyslexic academics who represented a variety of disciplines and who questioned whether the creativity associated with dyslexia should be confined to art education or whether the visual spatial skills dyslexic people often have, are used and indeed essential within all subject areas. Iain Biggs and Guy Saunders moved beyond creativity to models of imagination that are a prerequisite and central to the creative education process. Ultimately this was a conference celebrating the strengths of dyslexia and seeking to find ways to include these strengths within the academic community.

The Disability Equality Schemes which are now being developed require them to be informed by the experiences of disabled people. It is already clear from listening to dyslexic people that the experience of exclusion for people with dyslexia is far from over. I meet students who simply cannot find assessment strategies that do justice to their knowledge and understanding and who feel that their tutors do not take their difficulties within a text based academia seriously. I meet dyslexic members of staff who do not feel able or safe to disclose their dyslexia because of the sense of prejudice among their peers. Will Gosling, Alan Rayner, Mike Juggins and Iain Biggs describe the intense anger, frustration and grief associated with exclusion within academia and the sense of being an object to be studied and 'fixed' by those who work with dyslexia. David Pollak, Tim Miles and Ian Padgett describe ways we can begin to attempt to address this exclusion.

Several of the papers discuss the high representation of dyslexia within prison communities and challenge our education system to begin to address the exclusion within education that leads to so many disillusioned dyslexic people following this route towards social exclusion. The different styles and referencing of the papers reflect the different disciplines represented and reveal in themselves a contrast between traditional academic and the lived experience subjective writing referred to by Jack Whitehead in his paper "How can we enhance the flow of values that carry hope for the future of humanity?" Section 1 of the papers describes the study in computerised assessment for dyslexia funded by the WEBB Project. Section 2 focuses on intervention and the creative strengths of students with dyslexia. In Section 3 dyslexic writers explore creativity across science, art, dyslexia and education.

Jane Graves describes the power of imagination and creativity and the joy that is associated with the fleeting moment. She describes how sometimes this process can be excluded within our culture "However we define it I would see that play is our primary aesthetic experience, converting the painful into the pleasurable. Unfortunately, many adults have lost the capacity for imaginative play - possibly because our educational system knocks it out of us in favour of problem-solving - which is seen as more 'realistic'."

Ketaki Kushari Dyson's extraordinarily moving play Night's Sunlight has a vital message with regard to inclusion, yet, "The reluctance of people to take seriously a play translated from Bengali was quite noticeable. Wherever we went, we had small audiences only, and schools were regrettably the worst in persuading pupils and teachers to attend. As all our shows had to be one-off events in the venues concerned, there was no way we could lure the absentees back to the next show." The few of us fortunate enough to see this play at the Cascade conference found ourselves powerless to explain to others the quality of a message that is subtle, takes time to both say and be heard and has a depth that is central to our global culture.

Jack Whitehead's concluding comments describes the dialogue within the conference and carries the voice of attendees as well as presenters. There was a unanimous feeling that the conference needed to be heard more widely and since 2001 I have regularly received requests for more information about the event from around the world.

This collection aims to inform the many initiatives currently active in Higher Education that are questioning dialogues between art and science (eg. Transdiciplinary Landscapes 2006, www.projectdialogue.uwe.ac.uk), exploring visual and verbal communication (eg. www.writing-pad.ac.uk) and those seeking to develop access for a diverse learning community. It is for dyslexic learning support practitioners, for academics and artists interested in the relationship between dyslexia and creativity, for those involved in developing diversity in teaching and learning, for those interested in creative process and practice in academia and for those interested in hearing the voice of dyslexic people. These are uncomfortable issues that often ask us to sit in the difficult place between certainties, in between what often appear to be opposing magnetic fields. Witness the recent media outrage at Alexandra Davies' suggestion that Dylan Thomas may be dyslexic (Daily Telegraph, 1.09.06, British and Irish contemporary poetry conference, Oxford, St. Anne's College). Or the endlessly repeated forore over the latest "cure" for dyslexia or praise for the potential limitation of the gene pool. Dr John Stein describes the dyslexic gene as having a survival value (Behaviour Genetics, 2005), and the collection of papers here suggest we need the abilities that are often associated with this dyslexia. Jane Graves describes the suffering of those who are dyslexic and identifies that despite all our initiatives access is actually becoming increasingly difficult to HE for people with dyslexia because of the increasing focus on exams to "protect" from plagiarism. She describes a student finding the right words to describe his experience of exclusion, "You have dyslexia and those who don't will make you suffer for it". (Reverie and dyslexia, papers www.writing-pad.ac.uk).

We have to ask ourselves how we can address this suffering. How in our 24x7 driven society we can embrace the time to find moments of stillness where qualities which may not be obvious and which take a long time to emerge can be held, empowered, understood and expressed, sometimes without words. In my work I often say that the work of dyslexic people takes four times as long to emerge as that of non dyslexic people, but that when it does it is four times as strong. Dyslexic people often "go to ground" when asked to commit to the written word. The concrete permanence of words casts difficulty on the fluidity and interconnectedness of the layers they are trying to express. Many dyslexic academics have commented on the value of their having had tutors with the patience and confidence in their ability to allow their ideas to emerge over time, sometimes significant time. This book of the proceedings of the conference has suffered from precisely this difficulty, and I hope you will find the papers collected here reflect the depth and process that has led to their publication. I am deeply grateful to my colleagues for their patience. I believe that the publication of the papers collected here has never been more timely and will provide hope and essential guidance for the true inclusion of dyslexic people and their creative imagination and visual spatial skills within academia.

Morag Kiziewicz, November 2007

SECTION 1:
Identification of Students with Dyslexia

Computerised assessment of students for dyslexia: a preliminary report of an evaluation of the StudyScan screening and assessment suite.

Mary N. Haslum[1] and Morag Kiziewicz[2]

[1] Department of Psychology, University of the West of England, Bristol
[2] Learning Support Manager, University of Bath

ABSTRACT

The StudyScan computerised assessment suite for dyslexia was evaluated during an eighteen month trial as part of a collaborative project between three universities on the Learning Support services for students with disabilities or specific learning difficulties. Attrition and filtering of students from various parts of the StudyScan assessment process is described. The relationship between the intial QuickScan assessment and the main StudyScan assessment is examined. Preliminary findings from a validity study comparing StudyScan classifications and Educational Psychologists' assessments for dyslexia are reported. Ease of use of the StudyScan suite is discussed from both the students' and Learning Support services' perspectives. The study is being extended to increase the number of complete data sets.

Keywords: dyslexia, computerised assessment, QuicKScan, StudyScan, Educational Psychologists.

INTRODUCTION

The number of home based UK students with dyslexia entering Higher Education increased from 1,930 in 1994 to 4,964 in 1999 (UCAS statistics) and recent government initiatives in widening participation are broadening the spectrum of students entering Higher Education. The number of students with study skills deficits and literacy difficulties is likely to continue to increase as will the number of dyslexic students. The survey of the National Working Party on Dyslexia in Higher Education (Singleton, 1999) found that 57 percent of students with dyslexia are already known to be dyslexic on entry. This leaves 43 percent being identified and assessed in HE. In addition, application for the Disabled Student's Allowance required, until recently, a current (less than two years old) assessment of dyslexia. Already hard pressed HE Learning Support/Disability Resource Centres are experiencing significant increases in demand for their services both with respect to the identification of specific learning difficulties and the provision of learning support.

[1]Correspondence to: Dr. Mary Haslum, Department of Psychology, UWE, Frenchay Campus, Coldharbour Lane, Fishponds, Bristol BS16 1QY. Tel: 0117 344 4311

The current process for the identification of dyslexia in HE usually consists of an initial interview including a preliminary assessment. This may be followed by referral to an educational psychologist for an in-depth assessment, follow-up interviews to support application for the Disabled Students Allowance, advice on using the DSA and provision of further personal and remedial learning support. All this is costly in terms of both student and Learning Support services time.

A computerised assessment offers the possibility of standardised assessment and availability to all. If such an instrument were attractively designed, easy to use, valid, and reliable, it would be possible to adopt with confidence a process akin to the triage model of Accident and Emergency Departments. Students could obtain information about their difficulties very quickly and, if necessary, be channelled rapidly towards scarce learning support resources.

This screener + diagnostic model was adopted by Zdzienski (1998) in the development of the computerised StudyScan Suite (Pico Educational Services Ltd, 1997). It consists of a preliminary screener (QuickScan) which can be followed by StudyScan, a suite of tests designed to refine the QuickScan diagnosis of dyslexia (but not to supplant the role of the educational psychologist).

Not all students who attempt QuickScan will be dyslexic but they may still need further information and learning support. QuickScan is designed to cope with this by offering an identification of learning styles and indication of whether learning support would be helpful. Indeed the manual appears to suggest that the provision of information on learning styles is the primary aim of the package.

Sanderson (2000) examined consistency of categorisation from QuickScan for both learning style and dyslexia for five university students. Whilst the sample was too small to calculate test-retest reliabilities it is disturbing to note that not one of the five students retained their initial learning style categorisation on the repeat QuickScan, and four of the five changed their dyslexia classification.

Clearly a large scale reliability study is needed. Validity studies are also needed and to this end, the present study examined the use of the full StudyScan Suite. The relationship between QuickScan results and StudyScan results was investigated together with their ability to predict the results of subsequent educational psychologists' assessments of the same students.

METHOD

The data were collected as part of the WEBB Accessibility Project on the provision of learning support for students with disabilities or specific learning difficulties. This was a collaborative project between the Universities of Bath, Bristol and the West of England, Bristol, funded by the Higher Education Funding Council disability special initiative. The University of Bath Learning Support team took particular responsibility for the Dyslexia project, which was one of four projects on services for students with disabilities. The working group for the Dyslexia project was drawn from all three universities. The data for this particular analysis come from the Bath aspect of the project. StudyScan was launched at Bath as an integral part of the Learning Support Service, and consequently, data were available on many more students at Bath than the two other universities.

Participants
The QuickScan screener was completed by 126 students during the 18 month period of the study. This was preceeded by a six month period of system preparation and launch time.

The StudyScan Assessment Suite (Pico Educational Systems Ltd 1997)
StudyScan was designed as a computerised assessment instrument for use with students in Further and Higher Education. Its basis is the work carried out by Zdzienski (1998) for her doctoral thesis. The assessment suite consists of a "screener" (screening instrument) QuickScan which takes about 15 minutes to complete, and a much longer StudyScan assessment which contains a number of tests and takes between two and four hours to complete, although rest periods are advised.

QuickScan is a 112 item self completion questionnaire and was constructed using items from the Adult Dyslexia Checklist (Vinegrad,1994), and questions inviting self report of learning experiences, personal details and assessment history. "The QuickScan Report outlines individual learning preferences and study styles and includes personalised study guidelines. Furthermore, it indicates whether the student shows any significant possibility of being dyslexic and may result in a recommendation to go on to complete the full assessment in StudyScan" StudyScan User Guide 1997 page 3.

StudyScan is based on the SATA (Scholastic Abilities Test for Adults devised by Bryant, Palton and Dunn, 1991) which is an American test with nine sub tests and provides norms for 16 to 70+ year olds. Zdzienski (1998) adapted the test for UK students by anglicising the language, adjusted sub-test norms for a UK population, ran the full test on a group of confirmed dyslexic students and added tests of phonological and visual processing and working memory. She reports that the StudyScan outcome is based on a range of discrepancies, fluctuations in performance, and individual background information. The algorithm for computing the final categorisation, however, has not been published.

The StudyScan assessment consists of seventeen sub-tests. These cover non-verbal reasoning; verbal reasoning; digit-symbol coding; visual and auditory short term memory (digit span); visual short term sequential memory (snowflakes); vocabulary; spelling auditory; spelling recognition; silent reading and auditory reading comprehension; reading speed; writing speed; copying speed; punctuation; numerical calculations; applications of arithmetic.

Some of these are adapted from the SATA; some are SATA tests with modified scoring systems and some are additional tests. StudyScan was constructed using Rasch modelling. Internal reliabilities reported for sub-tests range from .599 for Application of Maths to .804 for Reading Comprehension. The lower reliabilities were attributed to the shortness in length of some of the sub-tests. Not all of the items fitted the Rasch model and presumably were removed before the commercial version was published.

In the printed report for each user, individual test results are given as raw scores, standard scores and histograms. The results are summarised in words and a dyslexia categorisation attributed. Finally, recommendations for different types of tutorial support and a synthesis derived from the QuickScan and the StudyScan results are provided. As yet, there are no published normative data.

Educational Psychologists' assessments

The diagnostic conclusions ("dyslexic"/"not dyslexic") of subsequent assessments of the students for dyslexia by educational psychologists were collated. Six educational psychologists were involved. Students gave permission for their results to be used in the study. All the assessments involved the use of the Weschler Adult Intelligence Scale (Revised) and a variety of reading, spelling and arithmetic tests.

Procedure

Students can approach the Learning Support Staff for help by telephone, email or by attending a weekly drop in session, telephone or email. They come either through self-referral or recommendation from a tutor. For the purposes of the present study, a first brief interview was conducted to identify the immediate circumstances surrounding their visit. If difficulties were presented which suggested specific learning difficulties, they were recommended to try QuickScan. A second meeting was held to discuss the QuickScan report, to discuss personal learning history and to establish immediate learning support parameters.

If the QuickScan report and the learning history suggested the need for further investigation, StudyScan was recommended. Some students were asked to try StudyScan if their personal learning history, rather than QuickScan, indicated difficulties associated with dyslexia. There was a further meeting to explain and discuss the StudyScan report. The discussion included explanations of dyslexia, the potential impact on study and academic achievement. Learning support and immediate support strategies were put in place and, where appropriate, students were also referred to other student support services. Once students had had time to consider the outcome of the StudyScan report, there was another second follow up meeting where queries regarding the StudyScan report were addressed.

UK undergraduate students who would qualify for the DSA (Disabled Students Allowance) were referred to the Student Money Service to enable referral to an educational psychologist. The educational psychologist's report was then followed by an assessment of needs. Each of these reports was discussed with the Learning Support service.

Each student gave written consent to their data already being used in the study.

The QuickScan and StudyScan categorisations were coded from the computer generated student reports; outcomes from the educational psychologists' assessments were also coded. Feedback from students and the Learning Support staff on the use of the computerised assessment was recorded and summarised.

RESULTS AND DISCUSSION

Filtering and Attrition

The study involved collecting data in three consecutive stages: the QuickScan screener, the StudyScan assessment, an educational psychologist's assessment. Of 126 students who completed QuickScan, 35 (27.8%) were identified as not showing indicators of dyslexia and 91 (72.2%) showed some indicators and were recommended to try the StudyScan assessment. However, only 66 of these did so. It can be seen from Table 1 that this attrition involved potentially severely dyslexic students. This is likely to be a problem for any such two stage process. Clearly care needs to be taken that as many students who screen positive in the first stage are retained for the assessment .

Nineteen of the 35 students filtered out by QuickScan, had evidence of difficulties in their personal learning histories and so were recommended to try the StudyScan assessment by the Learning Support Staff.

Relationship between QuickScan and StudyScan

An important requirement for any screening test is that should classify users as accurately as possible. It should demonstrate both sensitivity and specificity. A primary requirement for the

TABLE 1 QuickScan and StudyScan classifications

QuickScan Dyslexia Profile	StudyScan Dyslexia Profile							
	No StudyScan	Not consistent with dyslexia	Borderline	Inconclusive indicators	Mild Dyslexia	Moderate Dyslexia	Dyslexic	Total
Not consistent with dyslexia	16 45.7%	17 48.6%		2 5.7%				35 100.0%
Borderline dyslexia	3 42.8%		2 28.6%		2 28.6%			7 100.0%
Inconclusive indicators	3 27.3%	5 45.4%		3 27.3%				11 100.0%
Some of the indicators	13 27.1%	5 10.4%	6 12.5%	13 27.1%	9 18.8%		2 4.1%	48 100.0%
Many of the indicators	4 25.0%		1 6.2%	3 18.8%	8 50.0%			16 100.0%
Most of the indicators	2 22.2%				4 44.5%	3 33.3%		9 100.0%
Total	41 33.3%	27 19.5%	9 7.3%	21 17.1%	23 18.7%	3 2.4%	2 1.6%	126 100.0%

StudyScan Assessment Suite, therefore, is that QuickScan, acting as a screener, will identify potential dyslexics, and that StudyScan, acting as a more thorough assessment will not only refine that classification but also not identify as dyslexic any one not identified by QuickScan. To put this another way, for a screener to work effectively whilst false positives may be acceptable, false negatives are not. Given that the QuickScan results, according to the publishers, contribute 30 percent to the StudyScan results, false negatives should be fairly unlikely. The relationship between the two assessments for the students in the present study is shown in Table 1.

It can be seen from the first row of data that of the 19 students recommended to try StudyScan by the Learning Support personnel but classified as "having indicators not consistent with dyslexia" by QuickScan, only 2 were reclassified by StudyScan, and these as having "inconclusive indicators".

Twenty eight students were classified as showing indicators of dyslexia by StudyScan (mild:23, moderate:2, dyslexic: 2). Tracking the changes in classification from the QuickScan to the StudyScan categories along each row it appears that generally StudyScan had the effect of reducing the number of students with "indicators of dyslexia" but data on additional students is needed to make better sense of these changes. Overall, of the students classified as having "some", "many" or "most of the indicators of dyslexia" by QuickScan and who completed StudyScan, 26 out of 54 (48%) were classified by StudyScan as having indicators of dyslexia (includes mild, and moderate).

StudyScan and the educational psychologists' assessments
At the time of the current analysis, educational psychologists' reports were available on 40 students (Table 2). Forty percent of these were classified by StudyScan as dyslexic (includes mild and moderate), 20% as "inconclusive or borderline", and 20% as "not showing indicators of dyslexia".

Of the 16 students identified by StudyScan as showing indicators of dyslexia, 9 (56.3%) were assessed as dyslexic at an educational psychologist's assessment. This may imply quite a high rate of false positives but the StudyScan group contained mostly students with "mild" or "moderate indicators" and only 2 students with "indicators of dyslexia". Clearly further data is needed to clarify the situation.

In Table 2, 9 of the 12 students (75%) classified by StudyScan as having inconclusive or borderline indicators received an educational psychologist's assessment as dyslexic, and of the 12 students identified by StudyScan as not having indicators of dyslexia, 5 (42%) were identified by the educational psychologists as dyslexic. Both of these findings suggest a fairly high rate of false negatives.

For the moment it appears prudent to wait for further data which is still being collected. Currently there is insufficient data to carry out a statistical analysis on Table 2. Merging the top two rows for a 2 by 2 comparison using a McNemar Test currently yields a non-significant result (p>0.3).

StudyScan calssification	EP: Dyslexic	EP: Not Dyslexic	Total
Dyslexic	9 56.2%	7 43.8%	16 100.0%
Inconclusive/ Borderline	9 75.0%	3 25.0%	12 100.0%
Not dyslexic	5 41.7%	7 58.3%	12 100.0%
Total	23 57.5%	17 42.5%	40 100.0%

TABLE 2 StudyScan and Educational Psychologists' classifications

It should be noted that it may be inappropriate to treat the educational psychologists' assessments as that rigorous a "gold standard" as six different assessors were involved. The study is being extended to increase the number of students with both assessments.

Reports of ease of use

The advantages of using the StudyScan suite reported by the students were the anonymity and the speed of access to QuickScan, the short assessment, the brief report and the immediacy of feedback. They found QuickScan easy to use and felt it was informative. Most of those who went on to do StudyScan however found it exhausting. Many ignored the in-built advice to take a break at test 7 and soldiered on to the last test. Feedback could not be immediate as the writing sample had to be scored and entered into the StudyScan database by a Learning Support tutor.

There were some problems with the hardware and software, which further delayed completion and feedback for a few students and in some cases increased their anxiety and distress. The publishers and the university's technical staff were very helpful in this respect. The problems, however, highlighted the importance of technical support in maintaining a computerised assessment tool.

The Learning Support Services found the information provided on learning styles by the QuickScan report a useful way to start talking about specific learning difficulties with the students.

Several meetings with each student were necessary to support them through the QuickScan-StudyScan assessment experience leading to the conclusion that StudyScan in its present form could not be used as a stand alone assessment. A major concern was the amount of time involved for both students and Learning Support staff.

CONCLUSION

The study demonstrates the logistical problems of a two-stage computerised assessment. StudyScan was introduced as an integral part of the Learning Support Service at Bath and yet students who were 'potentially at risk of dyslexia' were lost from the StudyScan assessment process.

Students found that StudyScan took up a great deal of their time; some students returned several times to complete the assessment. Both students and Learning Support officers found the QuickScan and StudyScan reports overly complicated and time consuming to interpret.

There is as yet no published explanation of the derivation of the QuickScan and StudyScan categories nor of the algorithmic relationship between the two.

The study is being extended to increase the number of students with complete data sets. At present it stands as a cautionary tale for the evaluation of screening and assessment programmes with respect to the length of time involved to collect data when a number of different agencies are involved.

Currently, there is insufficient data to draw a firm conclusion about the relationship between the StudyScan classifications and the results of the educational psychologists' assessments.

StudyScan is an attractively designed automated assessment but there are questions to be asked about its ease of use, including the time it takes to complete, and the considerable input needed by the Learning Support staff, particularly in the interpretation of the results for the students.

It is an imaginative beginning for a computerised assessment for dyslexia, but at the moment, it appears that it will be dependent on data from first users for a while to come in order to refine the model from which its results and categorisations are derived.

REFERENCES

Bryant, B.R., Palton,J.R. and Dunn,C. (1991) SATA – *Scholastic Abilities Test for Adults.* Austin, Texas, Pro-Ed.

Haslum, M.N. (1989) Predictors of Dyslexia? *Irish Journal of Psychology* 10,4,622–630.

Nicolson,R. and Fawcett,A. (1998) *The Dyslexia Adult Screening Test (DAST)* London, The Psychological Corporation.

Miles,T.R. (1997) *The Bangor Dyslexia Test.* Wisbech, Cambs, Learning Development Aids (first published 1982).

Miles,T.R. (1999) *Dyslexia A Hundred Years On.* Second edition. Buckingham, Open University Press.

Sanderson,A. (2000) Reflections on StudyScan. *Dyslexia,* 6, 284-290.

Singleton,C.H. (Chair) (1999) *Dyslexia in Higher Education: Policy, Provision and Practice.* (The Report of the National Working Party on Dyslexia in Higher Education.) Hull: University of Hull

StudyScan (1997) Dublin, Interactive Services Ltd.

Zdienski,D. (1998) *Dyslexia in Higher Education. An exploratory study of learning support, screening and diagnostic assessment.* Unpublished PhD thesis, University of Lancaster.

Acknowledgment

Julie Littlejohn (UWE, WEBB Accessibility Project Coordinator), Christine Chubb (Bristol, WEBB Project Officer) and Jane Baddeley, Margarida Dolan and Philippa Kerin (Bath) were involved in the testing of the participants and, with Barbara Tull, in the provision of learning support.

Identification, intervention, institutional issues: A further view of the study scan project learning from student experience

Morag Kiziewicz
Learning Support Service, University of Bath

Identification

Pollock (1999) proposes in his paper "Dyslexia and Identity" in *Dyslexic Learners, A holistic approach to support*, that earlier identification of dyslexia, increased support for students with dyslexia in Higher Education and wider access for mature students may all have a bearing on an individual's sense of self. He quotes Ivanic (1998) who supports the social construction model of identity and discusses the construction of the "sense of difference" and being "other" as a consequence of difficulty with reading and writing. He suggests this experience has the potential for being compounded and further magnified as a result of a student's experience on entering higher education and again on identification and assessment of dyslexia.

The current model for the identification of dyslexia is based on the medical model. The presumption in "diagnosis" is still that it is the individual that owns the problem, rather than the learning environment to which the individual has gained access. One of the aims of the study into computerised assessment for dyslexia was to explore whether this had the potential to be a more social model and empowering to students for identification of dyslexia.

The ease of use of the StudyScan suite is discussed from the students' and the Learning Support Services' perspectives. It reflects the necessity for identification both for the person and the institution, balanced by concerns about the individual, for intervention which respects a student's sense of identity and for the impact of institutional issues involved in introducing a computerised assessment service on a university campus.

As described in the previous paper, Study Scan has two parts; Quick Scan is a quick diagnostic test aimed at identifying learning style and picking up signs of dyslexia, and the longer Study Scan diagnostic test is aimed at providing a profile of a student's cognitive strengths and weaknesses, at indicating dyslexia, and at making recommendations for support.

At the beginning of the project, Study Scan was widely advertised, both in Student guides, in all fresher student presentations from Student Support Services, and in academic departments. Quick Scan was available on the university network and instructions for its use were advertised on the learning support website.

In order to access the full diagnostic programme, Study Scan, Quick Scan (QS) has to be completed. The QS code is entered to obtain access to the Study Scan programme. Students generally found the programme for Quick Scan easy to use and enjoyed accessing it. Many found the questions a little puzzling, and in subsequent learning support discussions had questions relating to the laterality and kinaesthetic items in the test. Some students found a yes/no answer restrictive, saying they felt they could be both. Many were surprised by the left/right handedness questions and followed that up in subsequent discussion concerning ambidextrous and one handedness training.

Nearly all the students felt the identification of their learning style extremely useful and have found the guidance for their learning style helpful. Some students, who had experienced technical problems or had lost the first code, took the test twice. Occasionally this resulted in a different diagnosis of their learning style. This led to some discussion about which code to use for the Study Scan, and ultimately the student was advised to chose the code for the QS learning style report which they felt best related to themselves. Some students did come to learning support to discuss their QS reports, but did not elect to continue with the full Study Scan report, and some students who took the QS test never approached Learning Support.

Following discussion around the QS report, students were advised where appropriate to take the Study Scan test. This advice was based on a combination of the QS results and the early learning and family history. If the latter suggested difficulties of a dyslexic nature students were advised to take the full diagnostic test regardless of the QS results.

Study Scan requires that the student take a three hour series of tests for digit span, visual coding, auditory spelling, writing speed, accuracy and comprehension. The full diagnostic test can be left and restarted at any point, however this is not clear in the test and students were advised of that prior to starting. A break is recommended, during the test, at the seventh series of tests, at the time of the study a software fault developed affecting re-entry at the eighth test, requiring technical support from the makers. Students were advised by learning support to take rest breaks and food and drink, (which is not permitted in the library) however many students reported that they had worked straight through the test, and found it very tiring, but hard to stop.

StudyScan is held on three computers in individual rooms in the learning and library centre on the campus. Students could book time in these rooms at the information desk in the library. The test asks for hand written returns in a proforma for auditory spelling, writing and copying. Since dyslexic people frequently find forms difficult to use, students were advised to take paper and pen with them for these tests and to return these with their QS code to the learning support office.

Technical problems on one of the computers in the first year of the study resulted in a long wait for some reports to be generated and some students retook their QS and their full study scan tests in an alternative room. One student also had technical problems in the alternative venue and was referred immediately to an educational psychologist for report. These problems caused distress to the group of students concerned and added pressure to the learning support service, particularly since they occurred just prior to exams.

Intervention

The learning support tutor enters information from the handwritten returns the student completes while sitting the Study Scan test in order to generate the full diagnostic report. This is quite time consuming and requires particular attention to auditory spelling (for spelling consistency) and to grammar and sentence construction. The tutor-generated areas of the results can weight the synthesis of the test significantly, particularly in support recommendations, although consistency in the coding and processing results is retained. Technical problems can also occur, particularly with printers. Two reports are generated, one is the analysis of the tests, and the other is the Dyslexia report. Both reports come with a full description of the tests and the results. It is possible to print either of these lengthy reports (which provide far more information than is required) or to select the report information required for printing on a page by page basis.

Students were usually keen to know their results. The only difficulty experienced in meeting to discuss the generated report was usually in the level of demand for the service. Students reported aspects of the test they had found easy or difficult; many found the visual coding aspects of the test extremely difficult, however a few notable cases had determined coping strategies for the test and had unusually (and discrepant) high scores on this test group. Several found the maths tests difficult. There were occasional technical problems, for example sound problems, when the headphones had been left plugged in and students had not heard the auditory spelling.

In general, students enjoyed doing the test and many preferred the computerised diagnosis to the educational psychologist's assessment. Students also reported if they felt they had "cheated" for example used coping strategies such as making visual markers, or taking longer to write the free writing than the time they had been given. Most students evidently felt quite empowered by the experience.

As the study progressed, however, it became increasingly clear that the synthesis of the report and the recommendations made were not reliable. The histogram output which shows strengths and weaknesses for a particular testee was found to be a useful indicator for auditory, visual and coding discrepancies and the learning support service focused on these results in their subsequent discussion with the student. The Study Scan report was only used as a sole method for obtaining support where other additional methods were not available, for example for reasons of lack of time prior to exams or review, or for financial constraints for an international student. Where Study Scan was used as sole evidence it was always accompanied by a report and interpretation from the learning support manager. In the few instances where the Study Scan was sole evidence, the additional advice from learning support was accepted by the departments in all but two cases. Where it was not accepted, a subsequent educational psychologist's report confirmed the learning support advice and support arrangements were then put in place.

Students found the computer production of the histogram chart helpful and easy to follow, and the learning support manager used this visual means to assist in discussion of the report, and in the explanation of dyslexia. The discrepancy between the histogram and the synthesised report was explained, however several students returned after the first discussion and shock of seeing the results, having read the report, with concerns about the difference between the StudyScan synthesis and the discussion content. The histogram and learning support diagram tools were used to discuss the results in more depth. There was often recognition of difficulties on looking at the histogram results and these were useful in explaining the likely impact on study difficulties.

Where a discrepancy was revealed in the StudyScan report and further discussion of learning history also suggested difficulties of a dyslexic nature, the student was referred for an educational psychologist's report. As the study progressed, the learning support service was increasingly supported by the Student Money service in enabling these referrals. If the student would not benefit from an educational psychologist's report, for example an international student who would not receive DSA, or if the student did not at that stage wish to proceed further with the identification process, the DAST and BDT tests were recommended as an additional check for dyslexic difficulties. Learning support provision was put in place following identification through the use of StudyScan. The identification was made on the basis of the histogram, rather than the synthesis of the StudyScan report. Recommended strategies made by the learning support manager, were also based on the information displayed in the histogram.

A few students preferred not to go forward to the formal identification process, and some were reluctant at this stage to disclose to their departments, preferring to wait for the result of the educational psychologist's assessment before seeking alternative arrangements for exams and assessment. These students continued to receive some learning support.

Institution issues

The attraction of a computerised model of assessment for an institution is primarily resource driven. If the queue of students seeking learning support could be reduced by the student being empowered to identify their learning style, to find out themselves whether or not they have a specific learning difficulty and to receive automatic recommendations for how to study and address their difficulties, the resource savings would be significant.

This study identified that this machine model is neither possible nor appropriate, and indeed could create significant problems with mis-diagnosis and inappropriate intervention. The design of the computerised assessment had an inbuilt requirement for human intervention and the time resource commitment is potentially longer than a straightforward screener and referral to an educational psychologist.

One model that is current in some schools is not to bother with identification. This saves time and money: students report that they knew they were dyslexic and were given extra time for exams and some learning support when they were younger. However they were not formally assessed, did not know what the identification meant, nor how to work with their strengths. This is a false economy and a lost learning opportunity and results in expensive remedial work at HE level to address negative coping strategies developed as a result.

Another model, current in Further Education institutions, is that learning support personnel administrate a slightly more detailed screener/diagnostic tool to provide a diagnosis, however this assessment is not as comprehensive as an educational psychologist's report. This is not necessarily cost effective as the person time is significant, carries attendant risks of missing key difficulties and results in poorer information being delivered for the assessment of needs that ensures the student has appropriate support.

The utopian model is one where identification is not necessary and the learning environment is truly inclusive. Some schools and academic departments believe they have managed this, however learning from student experience it is clear that this is not the case. Furthermore the identification process, while time consuming and complex, does ultimately empower the individual as many case studies attest.

Conclusion

In the social model of disability it is society that disables the individual. In the context of dyslexia in higher education, the dyslexic individual is apparently disabled by the way in which information is presented and in the way in which an individual's knowledge and understanding is assessed. Ideally, we would not need to identify individual difference, and would seek to address the processing, delivery and assessment of content in diverse ways to meet diverse needs. In order to reach towards this ideal model we need to identify, quantify and value individual difference in order to reach some understanding of how the condition of dyslexia impacts on study and educational achievement.

The problem is whether we treat the symptom or the cause, and does it help to uncover the cause? In cases where dyslexia has already been identified, for example at school, many students thrive given alternative arrangements for assessment and appropriate support. Did they find the experience of identification distressing? The most usual response was "I was too young, I had no idea what it meant". Much of the support needed for students in higher education with identified dyslexia is an explanation of the condition, development of positive study strategies and appropriate tuition and equipment. In addition support is needed for the ubiquitous experience of damaged self esteem which often presents as negative coping strategies.

In students where dyslexia has never been suggested, far less identified, identification impacts on the individual and their families in profound ways. In case studies all the individuals had known they had always had a problem and had blamed themselves. Self esteem had been damaged at a crucial stage in development and a profound sense of loss of identity and separation from self was the apparently inevitable isolating result. The ensuing distress at uncovering the root cause was, in all cases, a grieving process. This process requires many months of support and encouragement to address. If students are not counselled through the process, identification alone will not support the student's development.

A major concern when embarking on an identification study is around labelling. The negative aspects to labelling are well documented and arguments against labelling are often accompanied by the ongoing "there's no such thing as dyslexia" or the "we are all dyslexic" prejudices that abound.

The key to the value of identification practice must be in knowledge of ourselves. Ownership of the identification process has to be held by the individual concerned. A medical model diagnosis is neither helpful nor enabling if it is not accompanied by information which assists understanding as well as by appropriate support strategies. There are many aspects of StudyScan which were helpful and useful but we would be reluctant to let any student use it without full support from the learning support service.

REFERENCES

Fawcett, A. and Nicolson, R. (1998) *Dyslexia Adult Screening Test*
London. The Psychological Corporation.

Miles (1997) *The Bangor Dyslexia Test.* Wisbech, Cambs,
Learning Development Aids (first published 1982)

Pollock, D. (1999), Dyslexia and Identity (in Dyslexic Learners,
A holistic approach to support, De Montfort University).

StudyScan (1997) Dublin, Interactive Services Ltd.

Zdienski,D. (1998) Dyslexia in Higher Education. *An exploratory study of learning support, screening and diagnostic assessement.* Unpublished PhD thesis, University of Lancaster.

Acknowledgment

Dr Mary Haslum, Department of Psychology, University of the West of England (UWE), Julie Littlejohn (UWE, Webb Accessibility Project Coordinator), Christine Chubb (Bristol, Project Officer) and Jane Baddeley, Margarida Dolan and Philippa Kerin (Bath) were involved in the testing of the participants and, with Barbara Tull, in the provision of learning support.

SECTION 2:

Supporting the Creative Strengths of Students with dyslexia

Celebrating Dyslexia, Maths and Music

Professor Tim Miles

Mathematical reasoning is a positive characteristic of dyslexia and this is important. One of my briefs is to celebrate Mathematics and Music and it's interesting that although these difficulties about subtraction, tables and symbolic difficulties cause great difficulty, some dyslexic people use their fingers, need concrete aids, need to count it up, all those sort of things, and are very slow and often very discouraged over Mathematics, and yet dyslexic people can be highly successful Mathematicians.

So you have this curious group of incongruities, with dyslexia. Some of the basics including learning the symbolism are difficult and therefore negative, but some of the other things, for example creative ideas are very very positive and this can clearly be encouraged. There are ways around the difficult bits, for example computers and enabling technology can do a lot as far as that is concerned.

Art and Dyslexia

Art from my earliest experience is a positive. Many of the children I saw who were experiencing all kinds of reading and spelling difficulties at school, they sometimes produced really beautiful Art work.

There is also Architecture and I think again there are physiological reasons for this to do with the two hemispheres and the symmetry of the two plana. This somehow seems and is still a bit speculative, to affect the balance of skills and one of the skills many of the Dyslexics seem to have is this holistic understanding, so they become Architects for example, can envisage things in 3-D and all kinds of ways.

I had a dyslexic Orthopaedic surgeon writing for the journal Dyslexia and he said he could somehow envisage the position of the bones, more than his colleagues could. There are many skills in that way and for those of us who are merely modal (as Professor Gosling puts it) I think I'm rather anti Dyslexic because they are horribly good at mending the car and mending the television sets and all those sorts of things, and folk like me are absolutely hopeless at such things, with great effort I did learn how to change a wheel when the car had a puncture, but you know it was very hard work, not the sort of thing I do naturally.

One of the contributors to Dyslexia and Stress who is actually a priest said this is actually embarrassing when the car goes wrong, "because I can spot it immediately but it's so embarrassing because I don't want to seem to clever so I simply got to let the others have a go first", and he could spot this sort of thing instantly. Incidentally in his chapter he said his room looks like a bomb site but he still knows where to find things, a lot of them are out in the open.

Computer programming is a positive characteristic for dyslexia, as is dress making. The skills which are thought, and this is still a bit speculative, to be right hemisphere skills. There is good evidence, but again a purist might take me up saying I'm rushing ahead of what's being proved, that Dyslexics tend to be weaker at left hemisphere tasks and good at right hemisphere tasks.

With my colleague Mary Haslum we had a chance to inspect some twelve thousand ten year olds. A sneer that really riled me in the early stages was that it was only the middle classes who were Dyslexic. There certainly were more teachers and more sophisticated people among the people I was seeing, but it was that they were more alert to the problem. But there were sneering journalists who said, let me quote, "If you live in Acacia Avenue you are Dyslexic, if you live in Gasworks Terrace you are just thick".

In this extensive study one of the things it gave me quite a lot of pleasure was to find we have all the social classes in our ten year olds including manual skills etc and in fact there was absolutely no difference in social classes, Dyslexia falls on all kinds of classes. We also took measures of handedness and my early cases were clearly right handed and right eyed. We found slightly more people who were partially left handed, more in the males in another survey and we need to exert caution in talking handiness and dyslexia.

Music and Dyslexia

The problem with Music and dyslexia is similar to Mathematics. If you look at Musical notation there is a large amount of information within a small space, and this means reading Music as with reading anything else Dyslexics are slower they take more time, and the actual sight reading is more difficult for music. However the holistic skills give great positive characteristics in music, such as composition, rhythm and playing by ear. There is a collection of essays by dyslexic musicians in the book, Music and Dyslexia.

This has implications, in particular the examining board have been marking students sight reading sometimes above their musical skill. Now this has been a real problem for us, they don't want to lower standards obviously, no examining board wants to lower standards. What we need to do is persuade all examining boards not to mark down the Dyslexic on things that are irrelevant to what you are examining.

If you are examining you have to decide if you want correct spelling or not, but if they don't want correct spelling then it is very wrong to mark somebody down because they are spelling badly. Similarly do you really want people to a particular job of work within a three-hour period? If you don't then you allow your Dyslexics (or anybody else for that matter) extra time so that you are not judging on how quickly they can get it done, otherwise the Dyslexic will panic. One lad I remember was doing an exam to do with vectors and he just got something reversed the wrong way round and only spotted this three quarters of the way through the exam. He had to start again, panic stations, and you get therefore the Dyslexic who fails the exam, yet they know perfectly well that they've got the understanding there.

If you are counselling Dyslexics I think the important thing is to have a good heart to heart talk to them, let them tell you what it was about the exam that maybe let them down. Maybe persuade your examining boards not to grade on so and so, or what ever it may be more continuous assessment. I'm not even sure about continual assessment. It is not as easy, although it might seem the obvious thing for the Dyslexics, I'm less sure about that.

I'd like finally as a celebration just to mention the names of those Dyslexics who have contributed to the Music and Dyslexia book. These are people who are successful musicians who were quite severely handicapped by Dyslexia when they were younger. Some of them are still fairly young.

Nigel Clark a composer, now Professor at the Guild Hall. Janet Coker again a beautiful singer, she's written a beautiful piece in the book, just saying books are my friends she loves books, she loves the feel of books and then when she gets this beastly musical notation, all dots and things, Oh dear I'm sure there's something lovely buried in there but I can't decipher it and she says I must learn to try and make written music my friend as well, it's a very moving piece.

There's a girl who had particular problems with Mathematics, Helen Poole; Paula Bishop who has been a singer, a very successful singer; Michael Lee who was a Double Bass player, he was very interesting because although they say that sight reading is difficult for Dyslexics, he said there is a paradox here, because if you are weak at something you just work and work and work and for whatever reason Michael Lee has taught himself to sight read, and doesn't have any problems with sight reading.

Conclusion

As we are celebrating I'd like to applaud Successful Dyslexics all the World Over. We've had plenty of them and this could be the celebration.

Finally I don't want to minimise the down side, of course there is a down side but I suppose the central message I'd like you to take away is if you are counselling or advising Dyslexics encourage them to be realistic, a realistic sense both of their weakness and in particular of their strengths.

References

Miles, T.R. (1982) The Bangor Dyslexia Test. Wisbech, Cambridgeshire: Learning Development Aids.
Miles, T.R. (1993) Dyslexia: The Pattern of Difficulties. London: Whurr.
Miles, T.R. (2001) Dyslexia and Stress. London: Whurr.
Miles, T.R. and Westcombe, J., (2001) Music and Dyslexia. London: Whurr.

Access to Higher Education for the mature dyslexic student: a question of identity and a new perspective

Dr David Pollak

ABSTRACT Using examples from interviews with mature students who are both dyslexic and from 'non-traditional' backgrounds, this paper proposes a new perspective which links models of academic writing with discourses of dyslexia and approaches to learning support. It relates this perspective to issues of identity, self-image and student experience, and concludes that the widening participation agenda needs to include a new way of construing dyslexic students.

Introduction

The Higher Education field is changing. We already have a much less homogeneous student population than ten years ago, and the likelihood is that the trend towards this will increase (Preece, Weatherald et al. 1998). Access courses open up opportunities for adults, many of whom did not realise in their younger days that they were dyslexic, to pursue academic study (Gilroy and Miles 1996). The Report of the National Working party on Dyslexia in Higher Education (Singleton 1999) points out that such students may not have been successful at school because there was not sufficient awareness of dyslexia at the time.

Initiatives towards widening participation (Dearing 1997; Fryer 1997) have led to the admission of more students who have not followed the traditional A Level route. We have more mature students studying part-time, and steadily increasing numbers of students who identify themselves as dyslexic (Singleton 1999), although as a proportion of the total student population this is probably well below the incidence of dyslexia in the nation as a whole (Morgan and Klein 2000).

However, the answer to this problem should not simply be a case of saying that 'Universities must do more for dyslexic students.' This paper will examine various models of dyslexia, academic writing and learning support which are offered to students. In order to illustrate the proposed perspective, reference will be made to interview data obtained from mature students (including two younger examples for comparison purposes) who reached University via a range of 'non-traditional' routes, as well as Access courses. These are people for whom entry into higher education is frequently a challenge to long-held elements of personal identity (Ivanic 1998); such issues arise for all dyslexic students and others who feel 'different,' but they are particularly salient for this group. Comments from students collected during a research project on dyslexia in higher education (Pollak 2001) will be cited, which refer to identification as dyslexic, self-image and learning support. The paper will also look at possible responses by the higher education sector to students whose sense of identity is challenged not only by the label 'dyslexic' but also by academic writing in general.

Table 1: Students who took part in the research (selected from Pollak 2001)

name	age	university	route	course	
Peggy	38	Spenceton	Access	Geography	
Fenella	44	Spenceton	Access	Social anthropology	
Victoria	50	Burnside	Access	Social work	
Susan	45	Spenceton	Access	Sociology	
Robert	31	Litherland	Access	Law	
Ron	41	Burnside	Access	Adult nursing	
Rachel	20	Litherland	BTEC	Occupational therapy	
Charlotte	21	Spenceton	BTEC	Social policy	
Adrian	25	Belleville	BTEC	Electrical engineering	
Mel	32	Burnside	HND	Education and IT	
Alice	37	Burnside	HND	Education	
Chuck	34	Belleville	APL	Engineering	
Lisa	50	Litherland	APL	Social/environmental studies	
Betty	49	Burnside	APL	Health visiting	
Charles	44	Belleville	APL	Building surveying	

The students who took part in the research (Pollak 2001) attended Universities in the North, Midlands and South of England; names of Universities and individuals have been fictionalised. See Table for a summary of basic information about them. (The abbreviation APL stands for Accreditation of Prior Learning.) Within this paper they will be referred to by these fictional first names:

Models of academic writing, dyslexia and learning support

Lea and Street (2000, page 34) set out three models of student writing, the second two subsuming the ones above them:

- The 'study skills' model – a potential student deficit in atomised skills; student writing as a technical skill

- The 'academic socialisation' model – acculturation of students into academic discourse; student writing as a transparent medium of representation

- The 'academic literacies' model – different literacies seen as social practices; students' negotiation of contrasting literacy practices; student writing as constitutive of identity; meaning-making as contested.

It is useful to explore these models in the context of dyslexia, because there are links not only between them and discourses of dyslexia, but also between the latter and approaches to learning support (links which also involve identity).

Lea and Street describe the 'study skills' model of student writing as viewing problems with student learning as a kind of disorder within the student which needs to be treated. Publications which adopt this model tend to present studying as a matter of technical skill; one states that 'studying is a skill, not a body of knowledge' (Williams 1989, page 'x'). The assumption made by this model of academic writing is that language is primarily a matter of grammar, spelling and punctuation, with these as 'autonomous, nonsocial qualities' (Street & Street 1991, page 152) and essay-writing a further set of discrete skills. If a student lacks these, s/he needs to be 'cured.'

The medical model of dyslexia (in which it is described as a condition which has symptoms and can be diagnosed) similarly locates any problem as lying within the student. From the earliest references to it (Kussmaul 1878; Berlin 1887; Morgan 1896) to more recent times (Critchley 1970; Hornsby 1984; Snowling 2000), dyslexia has consistently been represented as a biological deficit. The National Working Party on Dyslexia in Higher Education describes it both as a 'condition' and as a 'syndrome' (Singleton 1999). Students such as Chuck have held a medical view of dyslexia for many years:

> *I think dyslexia should be described as suffering, as in that the physical manifestations are bad – basically are bad wiring of parts of the brain – and subsequently it can be connected to a physical disability.*

In terms of models of learning support in higher education, the model which equates to the medical discourse of dyslexia is the disability model (in which students who need support are seen as having a disability which makes higher education inaccessible to them (Oliver 1988)). The funding of learning support in higher education is currently arranged, for those who qualify for it, by means of the Disabled Students' Allowance or DSA (DfEE 2001); many Universities place learning support staff within a Disability Unit (or department with a similar title). Information published for dyslexic students which adopts this model will often refer to 'students with dyslexia' as if it were a disease, and inform them of the need for a 'diagnostic assessment.'

Charlotte's experience fitted this pattern. First, the problem was presented to her as lying within herself: *'Spelling was picked up on terribly; grammar I was just slaughtered for.'* Then her tutor asked whether she had ever considered that she might be dyslexic. Charlotte was screened at University and told that this was indeed the case. She thought: 'Well, I'm dyslexic, there's something wrong; at least I'm not stupid and thick.' (Unfortunately this feeling was not supported by her Educational Psychologist's report, which quoted low reading and spelling ages and made Charlotte feel 'devastated.')

She was then offered learning support sessions with a counsellor in the Counselling and Psychotherapy unit. The 'medical model' of learning support tends to treat it as an exercise which takes place in isolation, with little or no liaison with a student's course tutors or subject context, although sometimes students prefer this (Keim, Ryan et al. 1998).

Universities which have refined their definition of 'study skills' have begun to focus more on student adjustment to learning or interpretation of the task of learning (Lea and Street 2000). Peelo (1994) uses this model; she describes a tutor marking an essay as 'a representative of an academic readership,' and states that 'the finished product must look like what passes for communication within that discipline' (Peelo 1994 page 74). This is what Lea and Street call 'inculcat(ing) students into a new "culture," that of the academy' (Lea and Street 2000 page 34). The academic socialisation model, in focusing on the role of a student's learning strategies or style in the process of acculturation into academic discourse, parallels the discourse of dyslexia which sees it as a 'difference,' or a constitutional developmental pattern of learning which does not favour an easy acquisition of fluency in symbolic material. Robert (as a former painter of architectural perspectives) and Ron (a former electrician who described being able to visualise easily where complex circuits fitted into buildings) both made it clear that they saw dyslexia as such a 'difference,' but they also showed the influence of medical models in their use of terms such as 'symptoms.' This reminds us that these models are not completely discrete, but inevitably overlap; they are distinctions imposed by the researcher on complex subject matter.

A recent HEQC discussion paper (HEQC 1996) adopted the study skills model of academic writing. It referred to the 'ancillary qualities' which a graduate should possess, numbering among these 'the ability to write in grammatically acceptable and correctly spelt English' (HEQC 1996 para. 14). The academic socialisation model treats writing as a 'transparent medium of representation' (Lea and Street 2000 page 35), in much the same way that the HEQC document does. It thus fails to address the issue of literacies as social practices. Lea and Street assert that under the academic literacies model, student writing and learning are seen neither as matters of skill nor of socialisation: they are viewed as taking place within institutions whose academic practices are founded both on power and on discernible discourses of literacy and knowledge-making. When literacy is seen as a social practice, or rather a variety of social practices, then the kind of literacy which is demanded in educational institutions becomes simply one variety, albeit one which is accorded supremacy (Street and Street 1991). In Universities which adopt what Street calls an autonomous model of academic literacy (Street 1984), students are expected to master a range of linguistic and communicative practices for different settings and purposes. The academic literacies model thus operates at the levels both of epistemology and of identity (Brodkey 1987).

The word 'discipline' is certainly well chosen, if 'correctness' in grammar, spelling, referencing and so on are seen as controlling and potentially discriminatory:*Insistence on correctness has a regulatory function in that it limits both the possibilities and the desire of many ordinary people to use writing to express their views (Clark and Ivanic 1997 page 215).*

This brings us back to the mature, 'non-traditional' higher education student:

> *A student's personal identity – who am I? – may be challenged by the forms of writing required in different disciplines, notably prescriptions about the use of impersonal and passive forms as opposed to first person and active forms, and students may feel threatened and resistant – 'this isn't me.' (Lea and Street 2000 page 35).*

I suggest that Lea and Street's proposition, which applies to all students ('dyslexic' or not), is particularly relevant to those who have not arrived at University directly from A Level courses.

This is because mature students may be in the process of changing their identity as they try to become members of an academic community, and this may conflict with other aspects of their identity (Ivanic 1998). Ivanic suggests that most mature students 'are outsiders to the literacies they have to control in order to be successful in higher education' (Ivanic 1998 page 68). This self-perception may be intensified by identification as dyslexic.

What discourse of dyslexia, then, matches the academic literacies model of student writing and University study? The head of the Computer Centre for People with Disabilities (University of Westminster) recently wrote:

> In terms of the social model of disability, I have always regarded the brain functions associated with dyslexia as part of a perfectly normal variation in the population, but the English language as a social factor 'disabling' dyslexics in much the same way as stairs inhibit those in wheelchairs (Laycock 2001)

Mel seemed to be groping her way towards such a broader view. She said that 'we ought to be more accepting of different styles,' and went on to talk about teaching everybody, 'right-brained and left-brained,' in a variety of ways. Were this to happen, Mel asked, 'would you be making the issue of being dyslexic almost redundant?' The students who took part in the research are part of a cohort of undergraduate interviewees which also includes students who reached University via A Levels; it was overwhelmingly this 'traditional' student group which provided the most confident espousers of dyslexia as part of the normal spectrum of human brain development (Pollak 2001).

Learning support approaches which adopt this kind of stand-point centre on supporting a student's self-awareness and sense of identity. All students need some degree of metacognition (thinking about how they think, learning about how they learn) in order to succeed, but those who are different from the main-stream need a particular degree of awareness of their own cognitive style (Krupska and Klein 1995; Given and Reid 1999). However, the difference between this and the 'academic socialisation' model (which involves concepts such as 'deep' and 'surface' learning) lies in the analysis of the University as a site of discourse and power. This is not a new concept. Radford (Raaheim, Wankowski et al. 1991 page 146) quotes a 1981 study (Ramsden and Entwistle 1981) which found that University departments perceived as 'allowing freedom in learning' had students with 'an orientation towards personal meaning in their studies.' Wankowski adds that there should be a 'feeling of mutuality in the social transaction of learning' (Raaheim, Wankowski et al. 1991 page 109). Student Charles needed what Wankowski calls 'the feeling of approval and recognition from another human being' (Raaheim, Wankowski et al. 1991 page 117) in response to his writing, and spoke enthusiastically about applying to develop his dissertation into an MPhil because his tutor had enjoyed working on it with him.

Learning support tutors who are aware of the academic literacies debate can encourage students to maintain a sense of self in their writing even while obeying the conventions of their subject (Creme and Lea 1997). Susan valued such work, which helped her to 'feel better about things and not feel so thick.' The model of learning support adopted in De Montfort's Student Learning Advisory Service (in press) involves listening to a student's ideas and working towards a way of putting them into an essay which feels right for him or her; this often includes acknowledgement of the validity of his/her natural sense of these ideas as a two- or three-dimensional pattern, and the fact that the hegemony of standard academic practice means that they must be shoe-horned into a linear order. This process implicitly requires counselling skills in staff working with such students, a fundamental element being the need to let the student know that s/he has been heard and understood. It is also possible to deploy counselling skills to facilitate a student's private challenge to the disability model of dyslexia, even though under the present system s/he may have to accept it publicly in order to obtain funding for learning support via the DSA (DfEE 2001).

Self-image and identification as dyslexic

The interviews with the students listed in Table 1 lasted for a total of 22 hours (Pollak 2001). There were very few occasions on which they deviated from seeing themselves as deficient as a result of being dyslexic. Whether they have heard of dyslexia or not, many mature students who have previously failed in education are afraid that they are lacking in ability (McLoughlin, Fitzgibbon et al. 1994). Victoria continued to worry that her difficulties were not connected with dyslexia, but rather the result of *'total idiocy.'* Fenella and Susan expected to be turned down at every stage, when applying for pre-Access courses, Access itself and then University. Fear that formal assessment will not indicate dyslexia, but prove fundamental lack of intellectual ability, is common to many students who are eventually identified as dyslexic (Miles and Varma 1995). The decision to re-enter formal education involves facing the issues of 'who am I?' and particularly 'why have I found studying difficult in the past?' (Riddick, Farmer et al. 1997).

For many on Access courses, the tutors are the first people they have met who recognise dyslexia and suggest formal assessment (Gilroy and Miles 1996; Singleton 1999). Ron took the initiative himself after struggling with an essay, telling his tutor:

> *Look, there's got to be something wrong here. I can't be this thick. I don't have a problem anywhere else. Why have I got a problem with this? Is it dyslexia, whatever dyslexia is?*

That quotation reveals several common themes: perception of dyslexia as a fault within himself, awareness of a discrepancy with other areas, fears regarding his intelligence, and patchy information about dyslexia. As they deal with people who can be expected to have trouble with academic study, Access course tutors are more likely to be aware of dyslexia than many other education professionals. This puts them in a good position to provide answers to these areas of doubt, but it also gives them great power to influence students' perceptions of themselves, of the nature of academic study and of dyslexia itself. For example, if an Access tutor adopts a medical model of dyslexia and describes it using terms such as 'diagnosis' and 'wiring of the brain,' a student's self-image may start to include the notion of deficiency and deficit.

However, the person with even greater influence in that respect is usually the Educational Psychologist to whom students are referred for formal assessment, as s/he has the kind of status accorded to medical consultants, and the role of formally applying the dyslexic label (Cooper 2000). Many Educational Psychologists subscribe to a discrepancy model of dyslexia (Turner 1997), and look for a contrast between a person's 'intelligence' as defined by a normative test and his/her attainments in other areas such as reading and writing. They therefore tend first of all to pronounce on a person's 'intelligence,' and for those who have been doubtful about their own, this can be a relief (Gilroy and Miles 1996). Rachel said that *it sounds like a professional saying you are OK,'* and Ron said *'I nearly fell off my chair'* when told his IQ figure (which was high). [The controversy as to the measurability of innate intelligence and the inevitable cultural bias of tests is not the subject of this paper, but must be acknowledged (Rothblatt 2001)].

Although the chief aim of seeing the psychologist is investigation of dyslexia, the issue of such labelling is contentious: as an explanation for a history of educational failure, it can be attractive, but it may raise hopes of learning support which will not be realised (Reid and Kirk 2001). The very label also places the 'problem' within the student, rather than within the institution. As Reid and Kirk point out, feedback to the student after an assessment should include a detailed explanation both of his/her strengths and weaknesses and of ways forward, as well as emotional support. For someone whose memories of schooldays include painful experiences of failing tests, such sensitivity will be essential during the assessment session; Ron, who was 39 when assessed, remembered *'walking past the door four times'* before going in, and being 'well wound up' by the tests. Learning support work also needs to start with acknowledgement of the emotional content of memories of schooldays (Raaheim, Wankowski et al. 1991).

These issues of identification are similar for students from all backgrounds. Gilroy comments that some wish to conceal the fact that they have been previously labelled (Gilroy 1995), sometimes because they hope to have a fresh start. For others, a life change such as enrolling for an Access course, with its new demands, may be the catalyst for the kind of exploration of learning approaches which leads to assessment for dyslexia (McLoughlin, Fitzgibbon et al. 1994). On the other hand, this point may not be reached until after the University course has begun. Having taken on the daunting prospect of a three-year course, itself a major change of direction in life entailing potentially major revision of self-image (Ivanic 1998), identification as dyslexic means that the student is informed that s/he is 'deeply flawed – or at least, that is how it is experienced' (Peelo 1994 page 24). Peelo adds that the label may seem to confirm a long-held feeling of being an unsuitable person for academic study. This may be compounded by the assumption that fellow students, almost all of course much younger, know the secrets of studying and have the mysterious skills. Such feelings apply particularly to writing, where initiation into membership of the higher education institution is often presented quite openly as requiring conformity to conventions of academic writing (Benson, Gurney et al. 1994); indeed, 'correctness' in writing can be seen as having a disciplinary, normative and discriminatory role (Clark and Ivanic 1997).

'Late returners,' as Peelo calls them, often arrive at University with a non-academic self-image, and may well over time have unconsciously built up a variety of ways of hiding what they see as their stupidity (Peelo 1994). If, like Lisa, they have come across television programmes about dyslexia, this may be compounded by feelings of anxiety about this as well.

On the other hand, completion of an Access course and admission to University may lead some students to assume that they have been deemed fully capable of completing their course (Singleton 1999), in other words already academically socialised. Various problems may arise as a result of this. Firstly, they may assume that their work must be of the required standard and hence that they need no support. Secondly, there may be an expectation of a continuing level of individual learning support which the University does not offer; Further Education institutions generally include a great deal more in the way of one-to-one support than Universities (Gilroy and Miles 1996; Singleton 1999). Thirdly, they may (in common with many students) be unprepared for the way the course becomes increasingly demanding from year to year.

A student's reaction to identification as dyslexic will probably depend on the way it is presented. Victoria's Educational Psychologist used what was clearly very much a deficit model:

> ......an endless list of things I can't do. No sequencing, nothing. Visual, auditory perception, is it called? That's all gone. There's just so many things wrong, I'm amazed.

In contrast with this, Rachel was told:

> It's just the way you are. It's not because you've been lazy or anything. It's something you're born with and it's, you just, you're just different, you interpret information differently.

Student experiences of academic writing (and stress)

Access courses generally provide guidelines on structure and argument, and most Universities offer similar documents on the technical aspects of writing. This approach is clearly within the 'study skills' model of academic writing (Lea and Street 2000). This does not help students with the much less tangible issue of 'tuning in' to the expected style of academic writing in their particular discipline (what Peggy called 'a way of portraying and receiving knowledge'), which in turn comes under the 'academic socialisation' model.

Furthermore, 'structure' in an essay involves linear thought, a left-hemisphere process (Krupska and Klein 1995; Springer and Deutsch 1998) which is often hard for a person with a preference for right-hemisphere processes (West 1997). Describing the brain in terms of this kind of preference is within the 'difference' model of dyslexia and thus again matches the 'academic socialisation' model of academic writing, which includes a 'focus on student orientation to learning and interpretation of (the) learning task' (Lea and Street 2000 page 34).

Victoria was acutely aware of what, she believed, was taking place in her brain; she was equally convinced that it was deficient, pointing vehemently to her head as she told me:

> I have trouble focusing, up here; I don't mean visually. Does that make sense to you? I can't get things into order. There's no order up here; it's like spaghetti junction.

(This is remarkably similar to what Susan Hampshire refers to as 'the ball of string filling my head' (Hampshire 1981 page 37). At times, Victoria added, 'it clicks' and she can 'see the road ahead.'

Peggy was conscious of the grammatical acceptability of her writing:

> *I still concentrate so much on my sentences, my words, the sort of overall piece of work is sort of, you know, still eludes me as a sort of run-on piece.*

Similarly, Betty spoke of spending many hours moving paragraphs around until the sequence seemed right, and moving words around until the grammar did so as well. Such a process often makes the 'non-traditional' student doubt her ability to work at higher education level; as Susan put it: *'I tend to think that I am not academically bright enough.'* Models which make students feel deficient are clearly not helpful to them.

Many dyslexic students arrive at University with deep-seated self-doubt, often derived from exposure to a deficit model at school, where they may have been labelled 'lazy' or 'remedial' (Gilroy 1995). Such feelings may be increased in the 'non-traditional' student. Fenella made frequent self-deprecatory comments:

> *But what was holding me back all the time, that feeling that it's ridiculous a person like me thinking of doing something like that when I knew there was something wrong with me.*

Such an attitude can often lead to 'helplessness' (Raaheim, Wankowski et al. 1991), and this may be exacerbated when feedback on early assignments conveys a message implying absolute cultural values and beliefs within the University which must be adhered to (Ivanic, Clark et al. 2000). Such values may be soon internalised. Susan said of an essay on psychology:

> *I managed to get 'excellent' for it and I spelt psychology wrong all the way through. That's totally embarrassing, it's unforgivable to do that.*

Another common response to the written work of a dyslexic student, when many versions and revisions precede the finished product, is to doubt that the author has any problems because the work is so good (Cairns and Moss 1995). Victoria expressed frustration with course tutors who were unaware that she had spent many more hours on her work than younger undergraduates, whom she perceived as able to write an essay the day before it was to be handed in. Victoria was voluble about the stresses of writing:

> *Panic! I do mean sheer panic. Put it away, have a wobbly, get the wretched thing out again the next day, have another wobbly, and then very slowly it can all start to sink in, bit by bit.*

Having begun to write, Victoria explained, **'the words take a very very long time to come forward.'** This may of course be particularly acute in examinations, where rapid information processing is called for, and other students are visibly writing at neighbouring desks. This is potentially the most stressful time for most students, but is usually more so for dyslexic ones (Gilroy 1995), and more so again for those from 'non-traditional' backgrounds who fear exposure (Peelo 1994). Charles had walked out of several examinations, commenting that his *'brain just literally locked.'*

Another potential source of panic is reading aloud in a group. Many dyslexic students may have had embarrassing experiences at school with this, but mature students are likely to have been at school in an era when humiliation and punishment were commonplace (Peelo 1994). Even if reading aloud is not called for, panic may arise in a seminar, when short-term memory and comprehension are simultaneously taxed. Mel explained this:

> *I developed the feeling like everybody's talking on a different level, it's going too fast, and I'm not, I'm not hearing the words, I'm not picking up what they're saying and I can't write it down, because it just comes and - like that reduced me completely. I had to sort of go out.*

In addition to the stresses of the course and of adjusting to the 'dyslexic' label, a mature student may have domestic responsibilities (Riddick, Farmer et al. 1997; Singleton 1999). As the short-term or working memory is often a dyslexic person's greatest problem area (McLoughlin, Fitzgibbon et al. 1994), carrying mental lists of family-related tasks may make it even harder to cope with a studying agenda. Furthermore, a feature of University life liable to be conspicuous to a student from an Access or BTEC course is that the staff do not provide a structure for private study (Gilroy and Miles 1996). In addition, pre-selected readings and digests are not often provided, and the overall quantity of reading expected is much greater (Gilroy 1995).Time management and personal organisation, frequently areas of difficulty for dyslexic people, may therefore be taxed; this is potentially a greater problem for those who are employed while studying.

Learning support

This is an area where students' experiences can be vary variable. At Spenceton University, which was using a medical model of dyslexia and learning support at the time, Peggy and Fenella were offered study support sessions delivered by a counsellor, whom they both experienced as preferring to focus on their emotional lives rather than their academic tasks. Nevertheless, there is clearly a great deal of emotional content to learning support; as Peelo points out, the first task is often to confront the issue of special arrangements (such as extra time in examinations) feeling like 'cheating' (Peelo 1994). Next, when examining learning styles and time management on a one-to-one basis, material about a student's domestic life inevitably comes up and this needs sensitive treatment (Raaheim, Wankowski et al. 1991). A mature student may have children to look after as well as a job to cope with, and as the dyslexic brain runs in families, one of the children might be dyslexic as well. For Lisa, it was taking her daughter to be assessed by an optometrist and a psychologist which had made her confront her own processes. She said: *'I suppose it was making me re-live what I had gone through.'*

At the time when the students in this study were interviewed, Litherland University had only just started to employ one part-time, sessional learning support tutor. Support for dyslexic students was seen as a welfare role, and they were assisted in claiming the Disabled Students' Allowance mainly in order to obtain ICT equipment. For Robert, this brought about a transformation; he took to voice-activated word-processing with enthusiasm, because he preferred to speak his ideas aloud, quite apart from his difficulty with handwriting. Peggy was also very positive about word-processing, as it allowed her to write out what she described as the 'little chunks' of her ideas and then cut and paste them. Victoria on the other hand hated cutting and pasting, because she disliked not being able to see text when it was on the clip-board; in addition, she felt that she needed so much repetition of keyboard procedures in order to learn them that it was quicker for her to write by hand. She did however like the way Burnside placed dyslexia support as part of Student Services, and thus on a par with the careers service, money advice and so on. (The 'non-traditional' student may be particularly aware of a need to feel 'normal.')

However, another feature of Victoria was her belief that she could not improve. Talking about her personal organisation, such as filing her papers, she said: *'Why waste my time sorting everything out? Things'll be no better.'*

Then she added:

> *Why won't my brain work, and say 'Victoria, this is how you do it'? Now why? Is this dyslexia, again? Or as I keep saying, is it total idiocy?*

Victoria seems to be a clear case of someone in need of 'reframing,' or changing the framework in which she views her own abilities (Gerber, Reiff et al. 1996). Morgan and Klein suggest that students' self-esteem can be markedly improved by helping them to see the extent to which their previous teachers were responsible for their educational failures (Morgan and Klein 2000).

Under a more social model, learning support tutors aim to help students to accept the person they are and what they can do, as well as what it is not worth trying to do. In some ways, this may be particularly successful when the support tutor identifies herself as dyslexic, which was the case at both Belleville and Burnside Universities; students were able literally to identify with the tutors. (This is probably less valuable when the tutor encourages an 'us and them' attitude, or a 'we dyslexics against the world' approach; if the tutor is dealing with her personal issues by making a 'mission' out of dyslexia, the results can be quite unhealthy.)

Victoria is also an example of a mature student who had the confidence to challenge her lecturers if they seemed to have forgotten she was dyslexic. She was indeed encouraged by her tutor to keep reminding them of her needs (such as having copies of overhead transparencies rather than being expected to copy quantities of text from the screen). Victoria spoke quite proudly of her assertiveness about this; however, the topic showed that her department at Burnside University was quite happy not only to place any problem within the student, but also to leave her with the responsibility to ensure she was taught in a helpful way. Rachel's course at Litherland was quite different; she appreciated the way one of her lecturers would write technical terms on the whiteboard *'in case any of you need the spellings.'*

Charlotte wished tutors on her course at Spenceton would be similarly mindful of the differing needs of their students. She hoped that her personal tutor would inform all her lecturers, so that she could avoid having to say:

Hi, I'm Charlotte W......., I started in your new course today and I just thought I'd like to tell you that I'm dyslexic.

'I didn't want special treatment,' Charlotte added; *'I just wanted it known.'*

Ways in which lecturers can help dyslexic students are summarised from a disability perspective in the report of the National Working Party on Dyslexia in Higher Education (Singleton 1999).

Conclusion: what we can learn from this model

Much of the above applies to all dyslexic students; however, the experiences of mature students from 'non-traditional' backgrounds help us to focus on the key issues. For any student, acceptance of the label 'dyslexic' means accepting that their difficulties are in some way the result of factors within themselves, often presented as disabilities. The dyslexia model can offer an explanation, but at many Universities it involves the student in internalising a deficit model of their own cognitive patterns.

The key to future progress lies in the attitude of the academy. Preece, though not writing about dyslexia, makes a relevant point:

> *The mass university no longer enjoys the protected autonomy of its old elitism.*
> *Instead it must respond to market forces and be accountable to society(Preece, Weatherald et al. 1998 page 2)*

Preece and her contributors argue for a different kind of higher education to accommodate new participants, and for 'the need to recognise 'difference' in both strategy and delivery methods if under-represented groups are to benefit' (Preece, Weatherald et al. 1998 page 6).

As we are now in an era of 'lifelong learning' (Fryer 1997), a problem which is going to need a great deal of attention in the next few years is the tension between academic rigour in assessment and 'student-centredness,' the latter being essential if 'non-traditional' students are to be supported (Johnston and Croft 1998). Jary and Parker list ten 'issues and dilemmas in the expansion of higher education' which have to be resolved; among these, they include:

> *Tradition versus change*
> *Excellence versus equity*
> *Exclusion versus inclusion and access*
> *Professional control of the curriculum versus student-led provision (Johnston and Croft 1998 page 4).*

Both Preece and Jary & Parker are writing about a broad inclusivity agenda, but the points which they make are relevant to the matter of dyslexic students. Dyslexia, whether defined as a neuropsychological 'condition' or as part of the natural spectrum of human brain development, confronts academic autonomy and oligarchy as clearly as any other aspect of the debate about widening participation.

At the time of writing, the Higher Education Funding Council is encouraging Universities to 'rationalise,' which in many cases means retreating from the heady expansion of the 1990s. Whatever their eventual size, Universities will continue to need first of all to recruit and secondly to retain students. As the National Working Party points out, 'many of the changes of practice in teaching and learning that are vital for dyslexic students can also be beneficial for other students' (Singleton 1999 page 169).

However, in the author's opinion there is probably a long way to go before there ceases to be a 'traditional' background for students to come from, and an equally long journey to the point where the autonomous model of academic literacy (and indeed the concept of dyslexia as a defect) cease to hold sway. Lea and Street (2000) conclude that the very notion of a learning support unit implies that students lack skills, and ignores their interaction with institutional practices. They add that for students, their own identity as writers is important; furthermore, is knowledge 'transferred,' or 'constructed through writing practices'? (Lea and Street 2000, page 45). These issues

> *are located in relations of power and authority and are not simply reducible to the skills and competences required for entry to, and success within, the academic community (ibid. page 45)*

A radical view is that eventually, reading and writing themselves will come to be seen as the skills of a medieval clerk, as advancing technology changes the cognitive make-up of 'dyslexic' people from an apparent deficit to a positive advantage (West 1997). Meanwhile, we have large numbers of people who are struggling to find a sense of identity as students in higher education; many are dealing with being 'mature,' with being 'non-traditional' in background and with being 'dyslexic,' and frequently with all three. The concept of 're-framing' learning difficulties/dyslexia by the individual (Gerber, Reiff et al. 1996) involves 'reinterpreting the learning disability experience in a more productive and positive manner' (page 98). Maybe the way forward lies in reframing by the University: a move away from labelling the student as having a 'problem' to seeing any such 'problem' as one for the institution. As Morgan and Klein put it:

> *This change in emphasis can be instrumental in allowing the adult student to re-enter education with a positive outlook. In response to the widening access to further and higher education, all teachers need to re-evaluate their approach to teaching to accommodate larger numbers of students with a wider range of individual needs (Morgan and Klein 2000 page 137).*

References

Benson, N., S. Gurney, et al. (1994). The place of academic writing in whole life writing. Worlds of literacy. M. Hamilton, D. Barton and R. Ivanic. Clevedon, Multilingual Matters Ltd.

Brodkey, L. (1987). Academic writing as social practice. Philadelphia, Temple University Press.

Cairns, T. and W. Moss (1995). Students with specific learning difficulties/dyslexia in higher education. London, Goldsmiths College.
Clark, R. and R. Ivanic (1997). The politics of writing. London, Routledge.

Cooper, R. (2000). Diagnosing dyslexia: a critique of the use of norm-referenced statistical methods and the case for an inclusive learning approach. The Skill Journal 68: 7-11.

Creme, P. and M. Lea (1997). Writing at University: a guide for students. Buckingham, Open University Press.

Dearing, R. C. (1997). Higher education in the learning society. Report of the Committee of Inquiry into Higher Education. London, DfEE.

DfEE (2001). Bridging the gap. London, DfEE.

Fryer, R. C. (1997). Learning for the twenty-first century, National Advisory Group for Continuing Education and Lifelong Learning.
Gerber, P., H. Reiff, et al. (1996). "Reframing the learning disabilities experience." J of learning disabilities 29(1): 98-101, 97.

Gilroy, D. (1995). Stress factors in the college student. Dyslexia and stress. T. Miles and V. Varma. London, Whurr.

Gilroy, D. and T. Miles (1996). Dyslexia at college. London, Routledge.

Given, B. K. and G. Reid (1999). Learning styles: a guide for teachers and parents. St Anne's-on-Sea, Lancashire, Red Rose Publications.

Hampshire, S. (1981). Susan's story. London, Sphere.

HEQC (1996). What are graduates? Clarifying the attributes of graduateness - a paper to stimulate discussion. London, Higher Education Quality Council.

Ivanic, R. (1998). Writing and identity. Amsterdam, John Benjamins.

Ivanic, R., R. Clark, et al. (2000). What am I supposed to make of this? The messages conveyed to students by tutors' written comments. Student writing in higher education. M. Lea and B. Stierer. Buckingham, Open University Press.

Johnston, R. and F. Croft (1998). Mind the gap: widening provision, guidance and cultural change in higher education. Beyond the boundaries: exploring the potential of widening participation in higher education. J. Preece. Leicester, NIACE.

Keim, J., A. Ryan et al. (1998). Dilemmas faced when working with learning disabilities in post-secondary education. Annals of Dyslexia 48: 273-292

Krupska, M. and C. Klein (1995). Demystifying dyslexia. London, London Language and Literacy Unit.

Laycock, D. (2001). Personal communication.

Lea, M. and B. Street (2000). Student writing and staff feedback in higher education: an academic literacies approach. Student writing in higher education. M. Lea and B. Stierer. Buckingham, Open University Press.

McLoughlin, D., G. Fitzgibbon, et al. (1994). Adult dyslexia: assessment, counselling and training. London, Whurr.

Miles, T. and E. Miles (1990). Dyslexia: a hundred years on. Milton Keynes, Open University Press.

Miles, T. and V. Varma (eds) (1995). Dyslexia and stress. London, Whurr.

Morgan, E. and C. Klein (2000). The dyslexic adult in a non-dyslexic world. London, Whurr.

Peelo, M. (1994). Helping students with study problems. Milton Keynes, Open University Press. Pollak, D (2001). Learning life histories of higher education students who are dyslexic. Thesis to be presented 2001. Leicester, De Montfort University

Preece, J., C. Weatherald, et al. (1998). Beyond the boundaries - exploring the potential of widening participation in higher education. Leicester, NIACE.

Raaheim, K., J. Wankowski, et al. (1991). Helping students to learn. Buckingham, Open University Press.

Reid, G. and J. Kirk (2001). Dyslexia in adults: education and employment. Chichester, John Wiley.

Riddick, B., M. Farmer, et al. (1997). Students and dyslexia: growing up with a specific learning difficulty. London, Whurr.

Rothblatt, S. (2001). Dare we toss out the test? THES. London: March 30th.

Singleton, C. chair. (1999). Dyslexia in higher education: policy, provision and practice. Hull, University of Hull.
Springer, S. and G. Deutsch (1998). Left brain, right brain. New York, W H Freeman.

Street, B. (1984). Literacy in theory and practice. Cambridge, Cambridge University Press.

Street, J and B. Street (1991). The schooling of literacy. Writing in the community D. Barton and R. Ivanic. London, Sage

Turner, M. (1997). Psychological assessment of dyslexia. London, Whurr.
West, T. (1997). In the mind's eye. New York, Prometheus Books.

Address for correspondence: dpollak@dmu.ac.uk

Dance, desire and dyslexia - Random thoughts on creativity

Jane Graves

Beginning to write this paper is like opening a Jack-in-the- Box' - which means I have no idea what is inside. All I know is that the title is 'Dance, desire and dyslexia'. So it turns out that the box is triangular rather then square. - which appeals to me. What I do know is that the following is not a closely reasoned argument. It is more like a walk-about. Already there are words written on the outside of the box, which continue to linger in my mind like a hidden wave in water. These are the words - spoken by the dancer Merce Cunningham.

'You have to love dancing to stick to it. It gives nothing back, no manuscripts, no paintings to show on walls and maybe hang in museums, no poems to be printed or sold, nothing but that single fleeting moment when you feel alive. It is not for unsteady souls.'

Hanging on to a fleeting moment is as disturbing as it is elusive. So summoning what steadiness of soul I possess I open the box and come across a statement from Freud which reads ' It is the transience of life which gives it beauty.' And I would add it is only through our creativity that we are able to be fully in touch with the joy and sadness of that ephemeral moment - the moment when we run the risk of being totally alive. Paradoxically, this requires us to be fully in touch with our mortality. The creative life is the lived life - and it cannot be lived without risk. Although dance, as defined by Merce Cunningham, serves as a sublime metaphor for its essence, creativity is protean in its manifestations. It cannot be confined to traditional creative activities. It is an attitude of mind rather than any specific action.

As a psychoanalytical psychotherapist I employ a psychodynamic model of the mind. In this context creativity comes into being when the unconscious comes into conflict with the conscious mind. The conscious mind is the one we rely on, the one that supports the comforting illusion that we are rational and reasonable. But whether we like it not the unconscious is the more powerful, making most of the decisions and doing most of the work for us - if we let it. The unconscious is outside time and space, so it's not surprising that we are mostly unaware of its existence. The deepest darkest part is completely dominated by the pleasure principle, demands instant fulfilment and cannot tolerate frustration. It is a chaos of wishes, unacceptable, contradictory, and incompatible, primarily powerful instincts of love and aggression in their most primitive form. It exerts a continuous and inescapable pressure on the rest of the personality. It is wordless and totally inaccessible. It is also the source of our drive and energy.

This is the Freudian Id. The id's constant attempts to emerge into consciousness are in fact very successful - but only in an indirect form. Repression is the strategy which consciousness employs to evade the id - but the id forces an escape hatch emerging through symptoms which the conscious mind does not understand. As I see it, these so-called symptoms are the ground work of our creativity. But it needs a creative encounter with an experience - sometimes with the aid of a therapist - to change this internal dynamic from negative to positive.

One could say, for many at least, that this radical change is an attempt to rediscover a lost skill - that of play. Regrettably, play is often seen as the prerogative of the child. Children play in the most dreadful circumstances - even in concentration camps. One could even say that play is a symptom which arises as a result of inner conflict - but one that is fruitful. Play not only links the unconscious with the conscious, but converts the most painful experience into the positive. In *Beyond the pleasure principle* Freud identifies the significance of the 'fort-da' game (gone - come back) in which his little grandson used a cotton reel on a string to deal with his mother's absences. This child of eighteen months threw the cotton reel under the cot (where he could not see it) and then retrieved it to prove it still existed. (Mother would return.) As Freud puts it 'Under the dominance of the pleasure principle, there are ways and means enough of making what is in itself unpleasurable into a subject to be recollected and worked over in the mind. The consideration of these cases and situations, which have a yield of pleasure of as their final outcome, should be undertaken by some system of aesthetics...' Or as Rilke says 'Beauty is the beginning of a terror that we are just able to bear.' Rodin expresses a similar sentiment with the phrase ' What we call 'ugly' in reality can in art become great beauty.

However we define it I would see that play is our primary aesthetic experience, converting the painful into the pleasurable. Unfortunately, many adults have lost the capacity for imaginative play - possibly because our educational system knocks it out of us in favour of problem-solving - which is seen as more 'realistic'. Secretly, however, in the dark night, most people have the chance to play - through dreaming. In our dreams at least we are all creative artists. What Freud identifies as the mechanisms of dreams, 'condensation, displacement, and symbolisation' - these are the very stuff of creativity. They not only conceal and reveal at the same time - but they give us the means of communication with ourselves as well as with others. Condensation turns the dream into a story - often an image. Displacement obscures the unwelcome unconscious meaning - and symbolisation means we can communicate with others as well as ourselves. Like Shakespeare's Bottom in a Midsummer Night's Dream we are wonderfully changed. Dream on!!

It has always seemed strange to me that Freud, who paid such a detailed attention to dreams - The interpretations of dreams is over seven hundred pages - should have been so cynical about the image when it seems so essential to many creative activities. Psychoanalysis was dubbed the 'talking cure' and many therapists continue to feel words are superior to images. It seems clear that Freud's empathy with literature was infinitely greater than his relationship with the visual world. Not only is this apparent in the quality of his writing (his case histories are brilliant novellas) but he would quote long passages from Shakespeare - in English. Given that until 1938 he lived in Vienna, the world of Klimt and Schiele, it seems even odder that his understanding of the visual world is so inadequate.

This bias was obviously incompatible with my work in an art and design college - and my encounter with dyslexia proved to be a wonderful corrective. As the dyslexic students flooded though my door, they changed me considerably more than I changed them. As they came to trust me they confided in me the power of their own internal imagery. I was asked by a course director to see if I could find out why a disturbed young man spent so much of his time travelling round on the tops of buses. It turned out he was sitting there with his eyes shut watching his own internal cinema! (This subsequently emerged in his very successful illustration work.) More sadly, another student who had desperately wanted to read physics at University said he could see and rotate images in his mind - but he couldn't cope with the text books. He could express his thoughts in diagrams and there really seems no good reason why examination systems at all levels should not offer this as an alternative mode of assessment. After all Einstein said 'If I can't see it I don't understand it!'

This capacity, to judge visual information as a whole and to change view-points in the mind, could be described as visual-spatial ability. It is commonly found in students who attend art/design colleges - and would seem to be the key to their creativity. It is rare, however, to find a visual artist/designer who is prepared to attempt to put it into words. Fortunately, a sculptor, Steve Furlonger, has given us a beautiful description of this aptitude. '.... sculpture shows me that we have the capacity to evoke imaginatively the world out there ...in here...coping with the external world and its vicissitudes, and these are triggered both consciously and unconsciously by image, narrative and correspondences.

It is more surprising to find a comparable viewpoint put forward by a scientist. Stephen Jay Gould, the evolutionary biologist, writes this of a fellow scientist. 'McLintock does not follow the style of logical and sequential reasoning which is often taken as a canonical mode of reasoning in science. She works by a kind of global intuitive insight. If she is stuck on a problem she does not set it down in rigorous order, write down the deduced consequences, and work her way up step by step, but will take a long walk or sit down in the woods, and try to think of something else, utterly confident that a solution will eventually come to her 'in extenso'. He goes on to say that he works in the same way. 'I never scored particularly well on so called objective tests of intelligence because they stress logical reasoning and do not capture this style of simultaneous integration of many pieces into one structure. ' What a wonderful definition!

I suspect there are many people with a similar thinking style - but I wonder if they have learnt to keep quiet about it. Which is strange in that these people may turn out to have an easy access to their creativity. Obviously not all of them would be diagnosed as 'dyslexic' but they might be said to have a 'dyslexic learning style' in the sense that they would benefit though being taught by the same strategies that benefit dyslexics. Certainly, teaching cultural studies in an art and design college, I found that videoing lectures, providing sets of notes and encouraging students to tape-record lectures benefited all my students - and indirectly me.

Nonetheless, it is still often assumed that verbal literacy is the end product of human development. This is part and parcel of a view of human development which sees 'humankind' (or perhaps one should one say in this context 'mankind' ?) as the ultimate in the perfectly adapted species. Darwin does not seem to have supported this teleological view. From the first he insisted that 'natural selection has been the main but not the exclusive means of modification' and Adam Phillips in his book Darwin's worms identifies Darwin's celebration of the essential role of the humble earthworm in making and sustaining soil. As Marx so aptly put it ' Nature is man's inorganic body'. I find Darwin's humility appealing. In the same way I am deeply touched by the concluding paragraph of Claude Levi-Strauss autobiography which begins with the words 'The world began without man and will certainly end without him.'

Not surprisingly I am enthusiastic about Stephen Jay Gould's view on the development of language. He suggests that literacy arose accidentally, through co-opting 'spandrels', areas of the brain which originally had no specific use - although he admits 'Reading and writing are now highly adaptive for human beings'. Even this statement is open to question.   For example, written history gives us one version of the past, but oral history, ritual and dance are alternative forms of remembering and celebrating. Carnival brings the individual into contact with conflicts between the individual and society. The Trickster who goes walk-about, exuberantly celebrating the oral, anal and phallic ecstasies of the body, reminds us of the joys of infancy - before we had succumbed to the pressures of pot-training and the loss of the breast. Such events also collude with the pleasing fantasy that in the infancy of the race there were no such pressures - an attractive myth!

Nonetheless myth is an essential form of play which helps us to resist an excess of conformity. And reminds us of dance - which is always now and cannot be recorded. It is not always understood that remembering also includes forgetting. We never know the whole of language at any given moment. As is sometimes said 'Language speaks us rather than we speak language.' In other words, language is like a merryground that we leap on to for a while before we fall off. So of course is memory - no matter if the unconscious and long term memory never lose anything,

This kind of thinking is much needed - and frequently undervalued. Unfortunately in the literacy game of the hierarchical society, Apollo rather than Dionysus, is ruthlessly re-established through the concept of 'intelligence'. It often seems to me that the educational system is primarily designed for failure rather than success despite repeated attempts to make education inclusive rather than exclusive. The recognition of a need for late opportunities - and late development - may yet help to challenge this. It is certainly good news for dyslexics who are often late developers.

I like to think of dyslexia as a healthy form of rebellion against destructive social pressures, a celebration of individuality - and, equally important, the ordinary. Rather than idealising 'superiority' and concentrating on special people let us think about and celebrate difference. To celebrate 'difference', is the first step in embarking step on a creative relationship with ourselves. And a creative relationship with others. We can learn to disagree creatively - meaning to hold two different points of view in our minds at the same time. In psychodynamic terms, this can be understood in terms of the Oedipus complex. As Ronald Britton defines it, observing the parents' relationship 'We can also envisage being observed (as well as observing.) This provides us with a capacity for seeing ourselves in interaction with others and for entertaining another point of view, for reflecting on ourselves whilst being ourselves.' It is only if through tolerating these alternative viewpoints that we become capable of self-development - by which I mean discovering and sustaining an individual learning style.

With this kind of thinking in my mind, it became harder and harder to stick to any straightforward definition of dyslexia - certainly I could no longer put my hand on my heart and say that 'Dyslexia is a disparity between spoken ability and problems with the written word.' From a negative point of view, the most consistent problem, and the source of most major difficulties was poor short term memory. On the positive side I found that my students often had a capacity to understand sophisticated ideas despite simplistic and naive expression of them in verbal terms. For example, poor word recall handicapped them particularly when they were anxious - as in presentations. Equally, they were frustrated when their rich thinking was reduced to banal commonplaces by an insensitive tutor.

And then I began wonder. Were they really so bad with words - or did it depend on what kind of words? Certainly writing course documents will hardly be their scene. On the other hand, their often bizarre word order can be turned to good effect. We have to remember that among the dyslexic are the poets and novelists - Keats and Shakespeare would make a good starting point. Anybody who could write

> ' If it were now to die
> 'Twere now to be most happy, for now my soul
> Has her content so absolute that not another moment
> Like to this succeeds in unknown fate.'

- this man, called Shakespeare, knew something about awkward word order! Despite its creative potential awkward word order remains one of the most frustrating symptoms of dyslexia. Putting it on an more mundane level, I think the student who tried to say 'Knee-high to a grass-hopper ' but ended up saying 'Chest-high to a knee-hopper' certainly had something going for him! But I don't think he saw it that way.

It is often said that dyslexics benefit from multi-sensory modes of teaching. This may be true for many of us. I sometimes wonder if there is a correlation between dyslexia and synaesthesia - defined in the dictionary as 'production of mental sense impressions by stimulation of another sense.' This experience is vividly described in Richard Cytowic's *The man who tasted shapes* or Vladimar Nabakov's autobiography *Speak memory* in which he recalls his rich Russian childhood in scenes in which every detail is omni-present. On most of my dyslexia workshops there is somebody who reveals themselves to me as being synaesthesic. On one occasion, when I remarked that some people think that Wednesday is green, a young man burst out 'Of course Wednesday is green. Everybody knows that! '.

I don't think synaesthesia itself can be equated with the creative process because it can be so overwhelming in its exactitude, stultifying rather than liberating. Something more has to happen - the magic whereby one sense is translated into another with such a vivid impact that it leaves us breathless. I am thinking of Shakespeare's 'Love's feeling are more soft and sensible than are the tender horns of cockled snails' in *Love's labours lost*. If you've ever touched a snail's horns and felt the horror of that impact, however gentle, as the vulnerable creature hides in its shell, you'll know exactly what he means. In terms of creativity it is not synaesthesia but an experience in which we smell a word, taste an object, see a voice, feel a silence which gives us access to the sensuous experience we need to access our most profound unconscious gifts. Proust's understanding of this is disturbing. In the final volume of his novel *In search of time lost* he describes how he had desperately struggled to find a theme for his unwritten novel. Accidentally, he steps on an uneven paving stone, and as he repeats the movement to the amusement of passers-by he was able to recapture the past. 'Almost at once I recognised the vision; it was Venice of which my efforts to describe it and the supposed snapshots of memory had never told me anything, but which the sensation I had just experienced, that I stood as on two uneven paving stones in the Baptistery of Saint Mark's had, recurring a moment ago, restored to me complete with all other sensations, linked on that day to that particular sensation, all of which had been waiting in their place - from which with imperious suddenness a chance happening had caused them to emerge in a series of forgotten days. ' Not surprisingly he called this final volume *Time remembered*.

Thinking about this, it strikes me that what is most profoundly important is the capacity to translate from one language to another - or even to speak two at the same time - in this case sensation and words. Dyslexics are usually hostile or indifferent to clashes between two different symbolic systems - for example words and images. I asked one graphic student how he coped with using words - and it became clear that he regarded words as a form of drawing. On the other hand, another student, who felt she was in the wrong subject area, said when she went into the room called words the light went off in the room called images. She could reverse the procedure - but she could not persuade the two to talk to each other.

Translation from one visual medium to another may be easier. It is interesting to speculate how dance, which is to me the quintessence of intangibility, can be interpreted in the visual world. I'm never quite sure how to read Degas's dancers. Is he celebrating the substantial middle aged woman trying to imitate the nubile grace of the young dancer? Certainly there is here a delight in the human body in its plenitude. Rodin's erotic sculptures for me, however, capture the essence of dance - a static sculpture which serves as a metaphor for movement, and liberates the inner spirit of many famous ballet lifts.

It may now sound as if I'm trying to abolish dyslexia. This is certainly not my intention. Nobody who has listened to the regular litany from those who have been called 'lazy' and 'stupid' systematically can feel any thing but moral outrage. As one young woman put it to me, 'If you have a problem and it's not diagnosed your personality grows round it.' A severely dyslexic friend of mine wrote a painful account of his fifty years of suffering, bitterly recalling his school days. As he puts it 'I overgot the red pen .....What no one seemed to notice was the imagination leaving the essays for the sake of safety. In the minds of teachers I was improving but I was getting lost and worse. For the science that was my love left me. There was luck coming through and things worked out not too badly in the end. I made it to art school and books and found escape. I still feel the loss of science'.

Recently, a taxi-driver described to me his beautiful garden which had been destroyed when the council demolished his flat. But he had resurrected the memories of the lost garden by creating stained glass windows in his new house. I expressed my deep envy of this and he responded by saying 'I was born in the wrong class - I love, opera, ballet - all those kind of things - but I 'm stupid. I can't spell.' I explained to him that there was a difference between a powerful visual memory and the kind of memory needed to retain and recall written language, and suggested he was probably dyslexic. It was a wonderful moment. Subsequently, we met again and he behaved as if he'd never seen me before - but managed to include in the conversation a reference to his dyslexia! This reminds me of a student who wrote 'Being told I was dyslexic was one of the most shameful but also joyous experiences in my life...It lifted the phantom 'D' cap off my head. '

Because I am a psychotherapist many people assume that I think of dyslexia as an emotional problem. I am well aware that losing a word, or a sudden attack of stammering may have an unconscious meaning. And sometimes students have told me that they believed their dyslexia had been caused by emotional difficulties. Two students claimed that it was the result of sexual abuse, meaning 'I can't read because there is something I don't want to know '. But, whether they were right of wrong, it can also happen the other way round. A middle-aged student, sulky, resistant and aggressive was referred to me because she was uncooperative. She had had a breakdown, in which she had become unable to read. As we managed to generate a dialogue between us I picked up on some confusing evidence. Finally, I diagnosed her as dyslexic. Almost overnight she became cooperative and friendly and started to work well. (She subsequently said that this diagnosis had saved her life.)

Moving from a prestigious art and design college to working in an underprivileged and horrendously deprived area has brought me in an abrasive contact with the brutal label 'illiterate.' It sometimes seems to me that every person who comes to address our local Tenants meetings begins by reminding us that we live in an area in which there is 22% illiteracy. I have no idea what how this figure is arrived at. How do we define 'illiteracy'? Nobody has knocked at my door asking me if I am illiterate! And I can't help thinking about the 70% in prison who it seems may be dyslexic. And we should remember criminals are tremendously creative - though not in ways that society finds very helpful.

This systematic abuse and contempt need to be challenged and addressed - if we are able to use our creative abilities positively. I personally regard 'laziness' as a distress call which needs to be responded to by therapeutic help - or in the case of dyslexics by appropriate teaching. Nor do I believe in 'intelligence'. Fine to celebrate difference - but don't let's arrange it in a hierarchy of superiority and inferiority. 'Stupid' is a term we use to abuse our enemies - like 'immaturity'. (In psychoanalytical circles it's 'underanalysed'). We're all of us abnormal - thank God!!

I must confess I think of dyslexia as an umbrella term. As a result, I have become more and more suspicious of a Government policy which continues to prefer a brutally hard-line distinction between the 'dyslexic' and the 'non-dyslexic' as I suspect it is a way of saving money - and a justification for failing to offer teachers at all levels the support they need. Nor would I see creativity as the exclusive provenance of the dyslexic. What strikes me as the meeting ground between the dyslexic and the non-dyslexic (assuming this is a reliable distinction) is that creativity only takes place when you can wipe the slate clean - 'forgetting in order to remember better.' For example, the poet Stevie Smith told me that she did the Times Crossword puzzle every day - but with the clues from the previous day!

What is remembering? Dyslexics are of course not the only ones with poor short term memory. They frequently have excellent long term memories, but they are handicapped by the fact that they have trouble in accessing them. In the consulting room the strategy for remembering is free association and this leads us into a new state of mind in which thoughts and feelings can talk to each other. It is often forgotten that certain thoughts are only possible at certain levels of feeling, and certain feelings only possible at certain levels of thought.

It is perhaps because of this that artists, designers, poets, novelists, dancers, all make use of this method of free association as a creative strategy. Major roles in classical ballet are usually passed on from dancer to dancer. It is the music that often serves as the memory bank and the stimulus for creative interpretation. Rhythm - along with rhyme - is one of the basic learning strategies. (This is why we teach our children nursery rhymes.) Poets rely on these skills to find out what they want to say. Many, though not all, write spontaneously and are as surprised as their readers to find out what it was they wanted to say.   In Keats words ' If poetry does not come as the leaves on the tree it had better not come at all.'

Memory may be located in the body as much as the mind - for how can we draw a distinction between them? I have in my consulting room a beautifully crafted wooden box which contains a secret - a cast of the Willensdorf Venus. This small figure with enlarged breasts and swollen stomach is usually interpreted as a fertility symbol. Fertility in bodily terms becomes symbolic in psychic terms. As we know, it is not unusual for artists or writers to think of their creations as children. Not only an endless chance of renewal but also the possibility of seizing at a chance illusion of immortality.

Dancers are blessed in that they are spared this illusion. It was assumed that as they age their greatest performances can only live in the memories of others, who may not remember the precise steps - but through experience or identification with the dancer's performance can enlarge their own creative being. Strangely enough, many dancers now continue dancing into old age, remembering and reminding their own bodies. Like Anna Pavlova they dance into eternity.

I assume that Merce Cunningham believes that dance cannot be recorded though film or video. Its glory lies in its ephemeral - and secret nature. In both psychoanalytical and aesthetic terms the most important mode of communication is unconscious. It is not just in dreams that the unconscious can communicate through powerful symbols. A symbol is something which is capable of being both itself and yet of representing something else. Individual symbols can be codified and developed into a language. When we use the term language we tend to think of the spoken and written form. But there are many different forms of language, visual, musical, and the multifarious languages of the body itself.

Gestures are a form of communication and we manage to say a great many things with them. Think of the wealth of meaning that can be conveyed through the twitch of an eyebrow! Gestures, which may be spontaneous are honed and refined in dance to a pitch of intensity and consistency. Indian classical dance is probably the most sophisticated physical language. Classical ballet has a crude sign language called mime - which is considerably less expressive than the dancer's dancing.

It is only the sign language for the deaf which can lead us into a comparable sophistication - as eloquent as it is beautiful. And according to Oliver Sacks it enhances the development of visual-spatial ability in the mind. Maybe it would be a good idea if we all learnt sign language as our first second language. I suspect that dyslexics would benefit would find signing a natural and spontaneous mode of expression. Sign language, like dance, liberates us into a 'Now ' in which joy and mortality go hand in hand - what Merce Cunningham calls 'the single fleeting moment.'

Creativity is certainly not confined to the dyslexic, but undoubtedly dyslexia can serve as a key to understanding something of the creative process which releases us from egocentricity and enables us to discover our proper place in the universe. Lacan writes 'The Emperor Choang-tsu dreams he is a butterfly. When he wakes up, he may ask himself whether it is not the butterfly which dreams that he is Choang-tsu.' It takes all our creativity to grasp our own bewitching insignificance. Few people have summed it up better than Stephen Hawkins when he writes 'The earth is a medium-sized planet orbiting around an average star in the outer suburbs of an ordinary spiral galaxy, which is in itself only one of about a million galaxies in the discernible universe.' So it no turns out that my Jack-in-the-box is a dancer, which has turned into a butterfly which flies away into a universe beyond my comprehensation. As Merce Cunningham say, such fleeting moments are not for unsteady souls.

References

Ronald Brittan ' The missing link; parental sexuality in the Oedipus complex in *The Oedipus complex to-day*, Karnac 1989 p. 87

Richard Cytowic *The man who tasted shapes* N.Y.Tarcher/Putnam/Saris 1993

Kevin T.Dann *Bright colours, falsely seen* Yale University Press 1998

Sigmund Freud 'On transience' [1915] in Vol. 5 of the *Collected Freud* by Ernest Jones ed. James Strachey, Hogarth Press 1995. pp.79-83

Sigmund Freud *Studies on hysteria* [1893-5] Pelican books 1974

Sigmund Freud *Interpretation of Dreams* [1900] Pelican 1997

Sigmund Freud 'Beyond the pleasure principle' [1920] in *Metapsychology* Pelican 1976 pp, 284,287

Sigmund Freud 'Ego and Id' [1923] in *Metapsychology* Pelican 1976, pp. 350-379

Steve Furlonger 'Myopic Inversions' in *Visual-spatial ability and dyslexia* Central Saint Martin's 1999 p.103

Stephen Jay Gould *The urchin in the storm* Penguin 1988 p.165

Stephen Jay Gould ' More things in heaven and earth' in *Alas poor Darwin- arguments against evolutionary psychology* ed. Hilary and Stephen Rose, Jonathon Cape 2000 pp.85-105

Stephen Hawking *A brief history of time* Bantam Press 1988 p.126

Claude Levi-Strauss *Tristes tropiques* Pelican 1973

Jacques Lacan *Four fundamentals of psychoanalysis* Norton paperback 1981 p.76

Vladimir Nabokov *Speak, memory* [1966] Everyman library 1999

Adam Phillips *Darwin's Worms* Faber and Faber 1999

Marcel Proust 'Time regained', [1927] *In search of lost time* Vol.6 N.Y. The Modern library.1999 p.255

Oliver Sacks *Seeing Voices* Picador 1990 p.95

William Shakespeare *Othello* Act II Scene i ll.192-5

William Shakespeare *Love's labours lost* Act IV Scene iii ll.337-8.

Marking the visual

Ian Padgett

Introduction

The three distinctive models of teaching and learning defined as "Frames of Mind" by Howard Gardner represent the evolution of education from the informal to the formal. His model can also be interpreted as representing a transition from an experiential or multi sensory system of learning to one which is almost wholly dependent on symbolic representation and abstract codification for its communication and reception.

Thomas West argues that contemporary educational orthodoxy privileges a minority of individuals able to make the necessary "neural dominance adaptation" (Geschwind, Gallaburda) required for reading, involving a single or limited cognitive focus, and that the insistence on this system of education may have been appropriate to the needs of the industrial revolution but not to a post-industrial age. Stephen Rose suggests that continuing evolutionary processes in culture and brain/mind adaptation may, given time, allow alternative cognitive processes and forms of communication to replace the dominance of the orthodox symbolic form.

We describe most classroom teaching as "talk and chalk", in higher education we have a requirement for an oral examination, the "viva voce". Unfortunately Gardner does not differentiate, in the "Intelligences" subsection of his theory, the cultural imperatives that led to the changing emphasis and to a written language as a dominant indicator for intelligence. He highlights communality in outcomes as linguistic and interpersonal in all three categories, in a) he indicates oral linguistic instruction, in b) oral versus books and in c) he completely omits oral transmission. We can deduce from this that the logical and mathematical become dominant at the expense of oral communication in the education process.

One of the most prolific and best selling contemporary publishers, Peter Kindersley of Dorling Kindersley Publishers, developed his business based on the juxtaposition of words and images on the printed page. He said "I realized there was a missing link between words and pictures. Words are incredibly slow and pictures are incredibly fast. When you put them together they work in completely different ways. We needed to find ways in which we could slow down the pictures and speed up the text." Not surprisingly, Dorling Kindersley Publishers were quick to seize the possibilities opened up by multimedia applications which enabled the spoken word to overlay text and image and which Peter Kindersley describes as "the most incredible breakthrough in terms of getting people to learn actively".

Historical context for the dominance of written language

Eco describes the way in which hieroglyphic writing is composed, in part, of iconic signs. "Some are easily recognizable such as eagle, owl, bull, snake, eye, foot, man seated with cup in hand. Others are stylized, the hoisted sail or an almond like shape for a mouth, the serrated line of water ..." He explains that these signs are ideograms that work by rhetorical substitution, "thus an inflated sail serves to represent the wind, a man seated with a cup means drink" and describes how the limitations of representing everything ideographically led ancient Egyptians to turn their ideograms into simple phonograms, "Thus to represent a certain sound they put the image of a thing whose name sounded similar".

Eco suggests that the discovery that combining different hieroglyphs created evocative visual emblems inspired scribes to "experiment with increasingly complicated and abstruse combinations, and they began to formulate a sort of cabalistic game based, however, on images rather than letters." The privileged group who understand their self developed code depart from the associative non-linear, un-sequential (potentially dyslexic) logic of the visceral or the intuitive and widely known. Later in history the political, social and intellectual hierarchies associated with power and control perpetuate the mystification and retain ownership of the keys to the code that have become synonymous with power. "The symbols were initiatory because they were wrapped in an impenetrable and indecipherable enigma, to protect them from the idle curiosity of the vulgar multitudes."

Kircher defined a symbol as "a nota significativa of mysteries, that is to say that it is the nature of a symbol to lead our minds, by means of certain similarities, to the understanding of things vastly different from the things that are offered to our external senses, and whose property it is to appear hidden under the veil of an obscure expression." Kircher understood, as Bacon and others had, that ideograms were universal characters referring to ideas, and not alphabetically to sound, confirming this departure from the experiential or tacit mode of expression to hieroglyphics that supported the assertion of a new order of dominance.

Contemporary research has revealed that Amerindians pictograms were a flexible pictorial language, which if allowed to develop might well have resulted in a language form that was not based on concealment. Unfortunately the social structures imposed as a consequence of imperial intervention inhibited this avenue of semiotic and transparent language evolution.

Kircher says "symbols cannot be translated by words, but expressed only as marks, characters and figures". One rationale for the mystification of written language is given by Umberto referring to Swift's imagining of "an assembly of professors bent on improving the language of their country" in Gulliver's Travels. "The first project, you will recall, was to abbreviate speech, reducing all polysyllables to monosyllables and eliminating verbs and participles. The second tended to abolish all words completely, because it was quite possible to communicate by displaying things (a difficult project because the speakers would be obliged to carry with them a sack containing all the objects they planned to mention)."

Ridicule and irony are powerful tools of political rhetoric. The Enlightenment had so subverted the notion of the natural to be the notion of the unintelligent that fables such as Gulliver were a complexity of paradox, that can be interpreted on many levels. It may be understood as a political critique or as social observation, highlighting the mutual incomprehension between the classes. The imperative to spread literacy was in part stimulated by a call for social reform and in part by the needs of the industrial process. Notions of improvement and progress required a subversion of the old order supported by a ruling class who were previously the minority and who held the keys to the code of written language.

Changing relationships between text, image and oral communication.

In the contemporary context we are forced, ironically, to consider the imperative in consumer culture of imbuing a commodity with social values. This new dimension to language has introduced the concept of 'product semantics'. Umberto suggests "this primigenial language should incorporate a natural relationship between words and things. The primigenial language also had revelatory value for, in speaking it, the speaker would recognize the nature of the named reality."

Cassirer argues that the non-mystification linguistic order sets an ideal that all subsequent creative endeavors not set in the context of formal language are doomed to failure. I would contest this in the sense that a linguistic departure from the descriptive into a symbolic representation only establishes a space for creative reflection. But it is not a cause and effect mechanism, an interaction with the metaphysical is possible through notions of the other, which differentiates mystification from the mystical.

Cassirer redeems himself in his conclusion to Language and Myth, describing the power of metaphor and stating, "although language and art both become emancipated in this fashion from their native soil of mystical thinking, the ideal spiritual unity of the two is reasserted upon a higher level. If language is to grow into a vehicle of thought, an expression of concepts and judgments, this evolution can be achieved only at the price of forgoing the wealth and fullness of immediate experience. In the end what is left of the concrete sense and feeling content it once possessed is little more than a bare skeleton. But there is one intellectual realm in which the word not only preserves its original creative power, but also is ever renewing it; in which it undergoes a sort of constant palingenesis, at once a sensuous and a spiritual reincarnation. This regeneration is achieved as language becomes an avenue of artistic expression. Here it recovers the fullness of life; but it is no longer a life mythically bound and fettered, but an aesthetically liberated life."

In his introduction to the exhibition, "Verbal Inter Visual" Chris Wainwright expresses the current state of developments, misunderstandings, and, by implication, transition of the "binary" languages evolution disrupted by the spoken word. He says "The discourse surrounding the relationships between text and image continues to preoccupy artists, writers and theorists, often fuelled by mutual dependency based on the need to develop, establish and question the construction of frameworks of meaning. Specific questions concerning the transferability, compatibility and equivalence of meaning between text and image, and their place in an historical and cultural hierarchy, are rehearsed in fierce academic debate and particularly in art schools."

Some of those aspects of compatibility and equivalence are highlighted in the reportage media, particularly where text is verbal commentary and image is real time and moving. Two examples come to mind where discourse is at odds with image and/or reality, one is wartime propaganda and the other is news coverage of events such as the miners strike during the Thatcher era. Both these examples have encouraged a cynicism about and disbelief in what had, until more recent times, been regarded as 'seeing/hearing/reading is believing', and the route to truth. Computer enhancement of newspaper photographs and illusory aesthetics in advertising have compounded our cynicism and compelled us to suspend disbelief. We now perceive the truth to be a movable feast and some of us have merged with the virtual.

Specialisation has, nevertheless, maintained and fostered a separate development or polarization of the language continuum through and beyond the Enlightenment. 'I am an artist, therefore I use a visual language. If I needed to write about my ideas I would be a writer' is a romantic and now broadly discredited view. However this binary is represented by a post-structural position where 'nothing exists outside of language and is therefore implicitly defined by it' which could be argued as being equally problematic as a framework of reference when encouraging visual forms. There are a significant number of works around which this, and other intermediary positions, can be explored.

The word is both spoken and written, the oral tradition where knowledge passed from generation to generation belonged, in the main, to nomadic lifestyles in the ancient world. In Genesis in the bible, God is described creating the world using the 'verbum', the Latin counterpart for our modern 'word'. The word spoken and the image made icon are the bread and butter of today's advertising industries. They stimulate illusionary lifestyle representations, suggesting individual or collective social change through consumer products. This development, initially promulgated by advances in photography, film and television is ever expanding, courtesy of the digital revolution in information technology.

Machluan's "the media is the message" has come of age. Contemporary high technology has reintroduced the importance and significance of the iconographic, not only in its message, but also in its systems controls. In the opinion of some this has generated a sub cultural debasement of English, for others it has liberated the language from the fetters of the elite literacy custodians of a language which has ceased to belong solely to English people, and which has become one of the global tongues for communication purposes.

I hope to indicate in the selection of references for this short explanation that I, and others, perceive that a wheel has come full circle in changing relations between text, image and oral communication. We may, once again, be about to embark on a period where the spoken word and the image become dominant in our culture. Perhaps it is already with us. Perhaps for ordinary people it never went away.

Speculation

We learn in ways, which utilise all our sensory receptors and demonstrate our receipt of knowledge through synthesis and externalization via our responders; the voice, the drawn image (in the form of abstract letter forms or pictures) and in a physical way (through gesture or body language). We express ourselves, and our expression is in itself a creative act. The creative industries in the UK are now the second largest industrial sector of the economy, both in terms of employment and capital turnover and investment. What then are the educational needs and imperatives in the context of this new situation, and what are the prospects for dyslexic people. Dare we suggest that dyslexia will cease to be a disability in the context of a society that no longer is driven by the written word and the need to spell 'correctly'?

There is a growing body of opinion leaning towards a view of the future which is more democratic, less elitist, in the sense that the dominant characteristic required for a successful career in the developing digital industries will not be those which are prerequisites for written language skills, as favored in Intelligence Quotient (IQ) measures and the orthodox examined academia.

Linear thinking has, for some time, demonstrated its limitations in the adaptive and/or innovative spheres of activity. De Bono expounded the virtues of lateral thinking thirty years ago. We are able now to consider this ability to reflect synaptic connectivity, mirroring the neural chemistry of the brain. Gardner refers to "Linguistic (less emphasized)" skills in his types of learning outcomes, reinforcing the growing dominance of the more holistic concept of 'communication' skills, of which writing is only one. The research project conducted by Steffert et al at Central St Martins, which evaluated the cognitive styles of almost 400 arts students, further supports the link between creativity and adaptive thinking to laterality and the synaptic, suggesting differing individual protocol in neural pathway development. These cognitive styles have also a predisposition toward the visual spatial.

If we are in new territory with regard to learning outcomes and requirements, are we also in need of a new critical framework with which to evaluate? Or are we dealing here with a balance of expressive forms, which have equitable values? This paper should be regarded, perhaps, as setting out an overview or a structure upon which to hang information which might help us to determine the answers to some of these questions. The Education sector, from primary to PhD, is undergoing a paradigm shift, but does this fundamentally change the evaluation of performance against outcome factors, which need to be presented in order to assure quality of educational experience?

"Something extraordinary must have happened to create human minds capable of producing the Altimira paintings" suggest David Horrobin. He continues, "What happened within our brains left no external trace on our bones, but it did leave tracks in the form of an explosion of artistic and technical skill. ...Artifacts show that human culture, instead of being dull, slow changing and near universal up to perhaps 100,000 years ago, became exciting, rich and rapidly changing, with immense geographical diversity. Something more than mere brain size must have been involved."

Horrobin's contention is that our modern minds were made by changes in the way nerve cells (neurons) inside the brain make and break the connections they make with each other. In some cases he states these microelement connections develop an extraordinary richness, which enabled skills to emerge never previously apparent. His main thesis is that "we became human because of quite small genetic changes in the chemistry of the fat inside our skull. These changes injected into our ancestors both the seeds of the illness of schizophrenia and the extraordinary minds which made us human".

This is a slightly different theory to many in the field of genetics, although Horrobin does affirm, as he develops his argument, that evolution needs both environmental conditional change and available novel circumstances, or a pre-existing genetic response, variation or mutation available when needed and labeled "exaptation". The relevance to our interest in dyslexia of Horrobin's theory is that he shows that relatively minute changes in the genetic composition and fat chemistry can bring about huge and dramatic changes in our neural pathway development, causing potentially huge leaps in intellect, but also for a tiny minority, conditions such as schizophrenia. While schizophrenia is a serious psychotic condition affecting a small percentage of the population, there exists along side it a concept called schizotypy, which, it is thought, may affect perhaps 10-20% of the population, including dyslexics.

The link with achievement and creativity is further stressed by Horrobin, as is the suggestion of an inheritance factor.

Conclusion

I would wish to develop this discourse at greater length in the future, but I am concerned to suggest at this point that it is my contention that individual cognitive styles are proven to exist and are long standing, for some 100,000 years. Social evolutionary change, prompted by economic imperatives and class dominance, have mitigated against most forms of expression and communication for most people. This is particularly demonstrated by the dominance of the linear cognitive style necessary for reading and writing, supported by the calibration for of Intelligence Quotient (IQ) tests, which are themselves a socio-cultural and economic construct.

Most individuals have developed coping strategies for the artificial and limited thinking style preferred by the 500-year dominance of this cognitive style. This has not, however, precluded the continuum of other cognitive styles within each individual, which can be represented by the astonishing array of so-called hobbies and the expansion of the creative industries. As we progress further into this new century, my opinion is that the pressure from all directions will support a move towards holistic communication and a redefinition of expressive response, both in the work place and in leisure. We will see a decline in the dominance of linear thinking, which will in turn require a period of transition where academic and other evaluative processes relating to quality assurance or measures of achievement will need to adopt notions of equivalence, until there is acceptance of like measured against like, understood to have equal standing.

During the workshop for Cascade, I presented marking papers prepared for a mini research project at Central Saint Martins, aimed at exploring equivalence measures for visual assessment, together with images and text attempting a full textual description of the images. There is a great deal of work to be done before we reach equivalence in assessment of "marking the visual" with the verbal, however the debate is current in Higher Education, and students demonstrating their ability in ways alternative to text has begun to achieve credence in a way never believed possible in the past.

Bibliography

Cassirer, Ernst (1953) Language and Myth Page references 98 (New York, Dover Publication Inc)

Eco, Umberto (1998) Serendipities: Language and Lunacy Page references 74 – 76, 87 (London: Phoenix)

Gardner, Howard (1983) The Theory of Multiple Intelligence

Geschwind, N and Gallaburda, A.M. (1985) Cerebral Lateralization, Biological Mechanisms, Associations and Pathology; Archives of Neurology, vol 42, Page references 428 -59

Horrobin, David (2001) The Madness of Adam and Eve

Kircher, Athansius (1650) Obselliscus Pamphillius II, 5, Page references114-120 (Rome: Grigani)

Rose, S and H (1999)

Steffert B., editor Padgett, I in (1999) Visual Spatial Ability and Dyslexia (London, Central Saint Martins College of Art and Design)

West, Thomas G. (1991) In the Mind's Eye (New York, Prometheus)

Dyslexics, drowning in the mainstream... Throw them a chance to succeed and not another spelling test

Mike Juggins

10% of the population are dyslexic. How do we level the educational playing field that provides the platform for their intellectual development? My name is Mike Juggins and I am a dyslexic artist and writer. The aim of this article is to re-focus society's view of dyslexia and education. The issue of how to secure alternative provision will then be tackled.

What is Dyslexia

Dyslexia is a word that suffocates and disguises the truth of a rather complex matter. Indeed, dyslexia is a clumsy term that is unkind as Dys means difficulty and lexia means words... therefore the focus is automatically negative by definition. It focuses on a small weakness of a whole mind set, rather than incorporating areas of intellectual difference, many of which are strengths.

You see we dyslexics are talented, socially disadvantaged and misunderstood. Taught through a method which leaves us confused and excluded from the intellectual development we seek and deserve. We exist in a place and in a time that sees dyslexics drowning in a shallow mainstream.

Dyslexia is a difference in the wiring of a brain and not as is suggested by *experts in the field* simply being "lazy" or "dysfunctional". But let's face it, some of these self proclaimed experts only ever get their information second hand. They will never really experience the difference in brain functioning in the same way as a dyslexic does.

The press often talks of re-mediation, cure and even eradication! Well it may come as a surprise but... I don't want to be cured, I want to discover and learn in the broadest sense of the word, not just forced to notate and regurgitate. Frankly, I don't care if my spelling is bloody awful as computers provide me with non-judgemental spell checkers. Often it seems that no other group in society is forced to over focus on their weaknesses at the expense of their strengths and their emotional equilibrium.

Unfortunately society insists on measuring our intellect by our inability to perform word-based tasks and chooses to highlight our weaknesses whilst often ignoring our abilities. No one individual is fully proficient in all areas of brain functioning. Physical and visual faculties are arguably more important than word based skills in many facets of modern living.

Current provision

Constantly focusing in on inadequacy will invariably adversely effect confidence and self-esteem. I believe that dyslexia is a natural and potentially beneficial difference and not a dysfunction? The plethora of strengths many dyslexics possess would suggest that this is the case. In fact there is a large amount of dyslexic success stories, despite the lack of appropriate provision through generations.

Dyslexics often have fluid, spontaneous, sets of natural strengths. They are often global thinkers, due to a more equal balance in size between the two hemispheres of the brain. When nurtured they are often able to see the bigger picture. This can often provide the dyslexic with unique problem solving skills that can positively benefit the whole of humanity. Einstein, Darwin, Eddison, Picasso, W.B.Yeats, Da Vinci, Lennon, Branson etc are all fine examples.

Why not change the shape of the wHOLE?

The present system causes emotional scarring, low self-esteem then follows. Despite having a higher than average IQs we often end up on the employment scrap heap or locked up in prisons. We are disadvantaged by inappropriate teaching approaches that never think to look at our preferred learning style and adapt accordingly.

Literacy skills would improve if the individual's confidence and motivation could be improved through better-suited multi-sensory teaching practices. We must to start looking at the whole person and not just their weaknesses.

Change must come

Presently we attempt to change the individual and not the system, as it keeps down the costs, in the short term. However, the human cost on the individual who is denied an appropriate education cannot be measured. Whilst the financial cost to society regarding the amount of unemployed and imprisoned dyslexics is costly in the extreme!

Solutions in the form of either a "twin track" system or separate state funded schools for dyslexics should be considered. These approaches would offer the type of teaching that is necessary to accommodate the dyslexic's difference in processing.

The twin track system would involve a separate multi-sensory (holistic) learning environment within the mainstream. This would complement the current teaching environment currently provided. Whilst a separate school for dyslexics in every LEA would also provide individuals with the opportunity to grow as confident people rather than ending up with low self esteem.

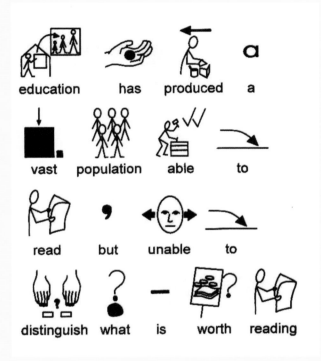

How would it work?

Changing the way we teach would have a profoundly positive effect. Acquiring Basic Skills are vitally important for all, yet dyslexics have difficulty learning these skills out of context. Subject areas such as History and Geography or Drama and English that overlap must work together whenever possible. This sort of change would motivate the dyslexic to learn across curriculum. It would enable them to link concepts and work on areas of weakness whilst simultaneously enjoying subjects whilst working on joint topics.

Providing more practical tasks and discussion opportunity positively effect dyslexics' ability to learn. Whilst extra literacy *remediation* often leaves that dyslexic feeling even more inadequate. In an understanding environment copying from the board and ploughing through text heavy books would have to be greatly minimised. They are a block to real understanding for the dyslexic. Information being relayed in mind maps or diagrams is more effective. These are all simple changes that would have such a emphatic effect on individual dyslexics. Virtually all of these changes would come at no extra financial expense!

Conclusion

The majority of dyslexics underachieve academically, unable to fulfil their full intellectual potential in the patched up, weakness focused system that presently exists. Change must come for all dyslexics and not just the lucky few whose parents shouted loudest. Or the adults lucky enough to receive good advice about what they are entitled to.

The emphasis must be on the system to match teaching method to learning style. It is no longer acceptable to place the pressure (blame) on the individual dyslexic student to always adjust. What we need is less fixing of the unbroken and more nurturing of the dyslexic's strengths by providing them with a suitable learning environment.

Contact details: mike@juggins1.freeserve.co.uk

Being Dyslexic in Higher Education

Professor William Gosling

I am going to talk about dyslexia and I had better start out by saying what a dyslexic is. This is not just anybody with any kind of reading or writing disorder, it is much more specific than that. I think the best thing I can do is quote Dennis Little, who wrote a lovely piece called 'Einstein's Mother' in a dyslexia online magazine. She's not herself a dyslexic but she's the mother of a dyslexic boy, and she says:

> "Dyslexics populate the world, the earth in great numbers they are all around us all the time: she's the little girl who forgets her lunch at home for the third day in a row, her jacket and her homework. It's the friend who gets lost driving in his own neighbourhood. She's the tour director that keeps saying 'go right - go right' while emphatically gesturing to the left, and the store counter who can't count the change. He's the young man who begins his chores in the middle and some how works his way out to the beginning and to the end. He's the guy rattling his tin cup on the bars of his prison cell. He's the man accepting the Nobel Prize" and there's been plenty of them."

> That is what I am talking about, I think Little might have added a bit more - there's some other pretty uniformly identifying characteristics she might have added that he will be almost certainly be wearing a digital watch, and he would certainly prefer Apple Mac computers to PC's".

Dyslexia was first recognised in 1896 by Pringle Morgan a GP in a paper published by The British Medical Journal. The existence of the syndrome has often been denied. In the past the sufferers were treated as mentally subnormal, uneducable or suffering from a moral defect. Once people even thought it was due to defects of vision and sometimes it has been attributed to defects of hearing. Both of these things are nonsense. It is in fact the case and has been established beyond doubt that the structure of the dyslexic brain is different from the modal brain. I shall refer to people who are not dyslexic as 'modals'. (Modals are all right actually, quite nice people!)

In the dyslexic brain the planal or temporal brain is symmetrical in the two hemispheres, which is very rare in modal brains. It is also known that the affects of injury, for example strokes, on dyslexics and modals are quite different. This very different brain development produces a cluster of different physiological and psychological outcomes, they include dyslexia – dyspraxia – allergies – left handedness – better than average visual abilities and enhanced creativity. Not all of these are present in every sufferer from dyslexia, if 'sufferer' is the right word, but a lot of them do they do cluster together. These differences in brain development seem to occur from the early months of gestation and are not reversible. The incidence of dyslexia is certainly not less than 5% and estimates tend to rise all the time, perhaps the incidence of dyslexia is actually rising, we just do not know. It is now thought that the incidences are equal between the sexes, although there was some early work that suggested that boys were more likely to suffer from dyslexia than girls but that's now thought to be due to bias in early research studies.

Like many, but not all, dyslexics I come from a dyslexic family. Not all dyslexics do, surprisingly enough, but many do.   My mother's, Aida, was dyslexic, I am dyslexic and so is my son Kerry, my daughter Melanie and my granddaughter Rebecca. Interestingly I am the only one who is left handed. Although this combination is common, not all dyslexics are left handed by any means. Patterns like this are fairly common in families, but anybody with any knowledge of genetics will be well aware that a simple dominant gene cannot explain these patterns. They simply cannot be explained in that way and I think they have a subtle and more complex explanation.

Let me turn now to my personal history. My father was an early amateur radio enthusiast and encouraged me to build my first crystal set radio, which I did at the age of four. At that time I also learned to read electronic circuit diagrams, which I did before I could read English. I taught myself to read English before I started school because I was intrigued by the writing on the sides of pencils and felt it had to have some significance that I wanted to pursue. My father, who was a thoughtful man, bought me a picture book that taught reading and writing and I boned up from that. It took me about a month, after which I began reading Henry Williamson's 'Tarka the Otter', the first book I ever read. I remember it to this day because I was in floods of tears at the sad bits. (If any of you have read the book will know that it ends very sadly). Tarka dies, and I was in floods of tears at that, but it also decided for me that I would be a writer. I wrote my first novel at the age of nine. It was a tale of lust and passion among fisher folk and was a cross between Mary Read and Arthur Ransome, it did not find a publisher!

At the local state junior school my reading was quick, my writing was execrable and my spelling was worse. I was told that my failure to solve my writing and spelling problems was due to moral defects and I was beaten. This did not work, so they beat me harder. Quite surprisingly, this procedure had great educational advantages for me because I realised my sensitivity to pain was not as great as I had supposed. I therefore stood up successfully to the school bully. At grammar school I became a boxing champion, which was just as well as I was hopeless at all other games - I'd never been able to catch a ball, nor have I had any interest in doing so.

Due to the disruption resulting from the aftermath of the Second World War, I attended three grammar schools in different parts of the country. My last move between grammar schools was six weeks before what were then called Schools Certificate Examinations, more or less equivalent to present day GCSEs. That change took place with a whole new curriculum. I changed from General Science to Physics, Chemistry and Biology as three subjects. I was written off by my school so I mugged up on my own and got distinctions in all three.

As a result of these experiences I became disillusioned with schools and I thought I could have educated myself just as well as they had done, if not rather better. However, I have to say that my attitude changed in sixth form when I was taught Maths. I was very fortunate, I was taught Maths by a remarkable man, Titus Thorpe, who was himself a dyslexic. He taught graphically, in pictures, using fundamental concepts rather than formulae, and established in me a life long predisposition to tackle all scientific problems from essentially visual first principle models. He also established in me the habit of mathematical thinking, which has never left me. I won a scholarship to Imperial College where, again, I was very fortunate because I read Physics under Sir George Thompson, a Nobel prizewinner and a dyslexic. He had a tendency to appoint dyslexics to his department - I'm sure it was unconscious - but I remember two of them particularly, Charlotte Kelner and R. W. B. Williams. When Williams introduced me to symbolic logic for circuit design and to Shannan's newly formulated mathematical theory of information I loved it. I decided to become an electronic engineer. Perhaps this was a triumph of early influences, I don't know.

I took all the examinations and completed my finals. In those days one had a long gap before one got the results so, as there wasn't much to do, I decided I would change my handwriting which, up until then had (as I said) been execrable. I read a book by John C. Tarr called 'Better Hand Writing', in which he advocated the italic style. I'd been taught round hand at school, as most people were at that time, a style very unsuitable for left handed dyslexics. I looked at Tarr's italic style and realised that it could only be written with a square nib pen, so I modified it so that I could write with a ballpoint pen and I changed my handwriting. I have to admit my handwriting is fairly artificial, but it is more legible than it was. Quite a dramatic change really.

I went into the aircraft Industry after I graduated, and spent five years there designing test equipment, latterly leading a small team. While doing this I thought I could see broad unifying principles in the design process, which were almost independent of what you were designing. This is the design process for complex systems. I encountered a remarkable book by Goodham MacCule, called 'Systems Engineering' and published in 1956 and, although I was very excited by it, I thought it insignificantly radical in approach so I decided I must write a book on the subject myself. It wasn't very easy to do that in industry so I moved to a university lectureship at Swansea and, at 29, I published my first book, called 'Design of Engineering Systems'. I then became a senior lecturer and I got the chair of Electrical Engineering at Swansea when I was 33. Subsequently I was Vice Principal, which is a curious Welsh term used in those days, meaning a form of Deputy Vice Chancellor. I was at Swansea for a while and then the University of Bath very kindly invited me to come and be the first Professor of Electronic Engineering, and am now an Emeritus Professor at Bath University. At the end of 1988 I was head hunted by the Plessey Company and joined the board as Group Technical Director and left them at the end of 1989 when they were taken over by GEC consortium.

I've done various odds and ends of things. One you might quite find interesting is my life membership of the Association of Old Crows. The Old Crows are an American Society obsessed with the idea of non-lethal warfare, and they kindly elected me a life member for inventing non-exploding mine fields, which is a great contribution in non-lethal warfare, as I'm sure everybody will appreciate. They're actually radio mines that stop you communicating if you go over them, so armies that go over them stop dead but nobody gets hurt. So they made me a life member. It was very kind of them.

I have written 15 books and I do an occasional column on science topics for the Guardian. I'm a High Church Anglican and I'm married with two surviving children. Well that's me. I've kept on writing books and probably still will, and got another half dozen in draft.

What have I learned about the problems dyslexics have in the Higher Education system? Well, as a student I learnt first that rote learning was difficult and unreliable for me. I could not plug numbers into formulae and get the right answers. I had to learn to derive everything from first principles, using pictures and diagrams wherever I could as aids. My work style was intense and I couldn't keep up for hours as my modal classmates claimed they could. After 20 minutes I had to take a break for 10 minutes. However, the intensity of concentration was such that I was oblivious of all around me while working - for 20 years I had no study or personal work space at all, and worked at a table writing my books in the busiest room in the house.

I have always been a clumsy and unsuccessful experimentalist all my life - my research students used to try and keep me away from their equipment - but I could get hold of supposedly difficult abstract ideas and generalisations without trouble. I had little chance of remembering the names of my fellow students or colleagues, that's been a problem all my working life, but I've got vivid mental images of pages from journals and texts books from 50 years ago.

When I began to lecture my visual memory was a stumbling block. I didn't realise that I was different from other people in this respect. I would put up complicated diagrams on the screen or blackboard and take them away again quite quickly and I didn't realise that my students couldn't still see them. So I would keep on lecturing about them and they would seem to be rather puzzled by this. I soon learned to give them a little more time to make full copies. In tutorials I could only show students how to derive solutions to problems from first principles, I was never able formally to record, or even name, important theorems, and I suspect some of the modal students despised me for that - I saw it in their eyes - and they often wondered how I became appointed. (So did I, to be honest). I often disconcerted students by proposing off-beat and non-standard solutions to problems which were not in the textbooks, often shorter than the ones in the textbooks. Some students came to like this, while others did not. Well they were better off with another tutor, a modal thinker.

When I write my lecture notes, articles or books, the ordering is the stumbling block. The order of words in sentences, of sentences in paragraphs and paragraphs in chapters, and even of chapters in a complete book, is a problem. Everything I need to say is there, but often quite jumbled, as though I hold the whole thing in my mind but all of it simultaneously and each element coexistent. The only solution to this I have learned is to get the thing onto the computer screen in whatever order it comes and then sort the order out later.
I typically redraft at least a dozen times, mostly changing the order of things. Thank God for the word processor, which makes this easy.

What advice do I have for dyslexic academics? Simply this:
Break a probable life-long habit of hiding your dyslexia. Make a stand as a dyslexic. Take pride in, rather than being ashamed of, being dyslexic. Come out of the closet and show your pride in being a dyslexic. In all universities we need dyslexics.

I also believe that university departments have certain duties. I think first of all departments have to come to terms with the reality that there are two kinds of minds in this world. (There are probably more than two, but certainly this is not as important an issue). There is the dyslexic and the modal mind - both merit full respect and nobody can transform one into the other. (Beatings don't work!). I think departments should encourage their dyslexic staff members, since any large department is likely to have some, to come out and identify themselves because it needs them to help the students. I also think you should warn dyslexic potential students at admission if you don't have any dyslexic teaching colleagues so the applicants can seriously consider where they would prefer to be educated amongst their own kind. (I know this is a very controversial view). You should encourage dyslexic colleagues to work with dyslexic students so that like can talk to like. I think these simple rules would make life a lot easier. I benefited by that sort of thing myself by pure chance and I think lots of others could benefit by it.

In conclusion I want to say is that there have always been dyslexics in human history and they have played a valuable, perhaps an indispensable, role. Let me illustrate this with just a few names of known or suspected dyslexics.
Augusta Aida, Countess of Lovelace, who wrote the first computer programme and is regarded as the inventor of software; Anthony Andrews, Hans Christian Anderson, Richard Branson, entrepreneur business man, Agatha Christie, Winston Churchill, Charles Darwin, Thomas Alver Edison, Albert Einstein (Einstein couldn't tie his shoelaces until he was nine), Whoopi Goldberg, Susan Hampshire, Michael Heseltine, Anthony Hopkins, John Lennon, James Clarke Maxwell, probably the greatest theoretical physicist who ever lived and who was dismissed from his post at the University of Aberdeen because he couldn't spell, eventually going on to Cambridge to lay the foundations of theoretical physics. Nicholas Negrapondy, Richard Rodgers, famous architect, Jackie Stewart and William Butler-Yeats

Just a few names, there are many more.

Theoretical biology suggests that the presence of dyslexics has survival value for human beings. Culturally, their creative presence has enriched human society. However, a world with nothing but dyslexics would teeter on the brink of disaster. The modals do far better at very many things that we dyslexics do not excel in. If you doubt my word try buying a computer direct from Apple, a company almost entirely staffed by dyslexics. I ordered one six months ago and its been delivered three times so far. They keep saying: "God, we've forgotten to send him his computer"! So we need the modals, we dyslexic people need the modals. But I think the modals also need us. So from both sides of this divide let us value each other, each trying to do our best; going forth in mutual respect and fruitful partnership.

How can we enhance the flow of values that carry hope for the future of humanity? (Part I)

Dr Jack Whitehead

This is largely an edited transcript of the conclusion to the conference presented by Jack Whitehead. To begin with Jack showed a video clip of himself with Je Kan Adler-Collins a PhD student who is dyslexic. He describes how he is working with the student and does not initially pick up on his emotional state. Referring to the point made by Guy Saunders about the artist's 'wonderful look of astonishment when a creative moment is reached', Jack showed how that microsecond emotion is actually experienced in his art as an educator. "I think that is what I try to do with my students – they are trying to give a form to their lives in a way their embodied values are lived as fully as they can be. In our often rigorous and valid forms of education this is often very difficult to put into words, and I believe this is what dyslexia in education is essentially about."

Jack showed how his interest in multi media and use of the digital camera enables him to go through each minute clip. "It is such a valuable tool and such a powerful experience to go through and see what it is I am doing, second by second, picking up body language, facial expression – there is a particular moment where I inappropriately laugh uproariously. I become aware of my own art, and the things that I do that I could not have planned that can switch it" that is a negative situation, to one that is positive.

The clip showed the student's frustration, "I'm irritated that the very people stopping me from sharing my experiences ... are couch potatoes. I'm not an ego maniac – I'm irritated, I'm tired, I'm in pain ... I've done everything, I've been all around the block and I've jumped through every hoop, but I'm so tired. You're saying I'm being disparaging – I'm angry". Jack says "All right, you're angry." The clip shows that there is a moment where the student is angry with Jack and all that he represents in education. Angry with the suggestions that Jack is making and frustrated, he says "why can't I be justifiably angry in the text?"

Jack suggests a way "that offers a more accepting attitude towards the unknown. This (suggestion) opens that for you - a better way in relation to a critical reflective story". The student asks "How would that stand up against the academics that think it's a load of nonsense?" Jack replies, "This is the academic (referring to his book on the Growth of Educational Knowledge) , it was written in about '92, and is quoting other research 10 years ago. All I'm saying is this opens up the opportunity to justify what you are doing – I know you may not wish to justify, but it is a very powerful way."

Then the clip shows the transition from anger and frustration to mutual understanding. The student says, "So you suggest bring that in earlier in my methodology will be" Jack replies,

"Exactly". The student responds, "Well, I'd better take that out. I've lost a quote, I've lost a reference. This is the end, I can do anything else, but not lose my references." But both Jack and the student are laughing together now and the transition to mutual understanding and acceptance has been made. These ideas have continued to develop since our Cascade Conference and can be viewed in the living-action-research e-Forum developed by Je Kan Adler Collins (1)

Jack showed how, in terms of the processes of learning that he hopes to promote those moments cannot be planned. Yet if you get video images you can start to represent some of those influences you have and relationships to people you are with. "The pleasure for me is that his dissertation, which as a dyslexic he really did have some problems representing his enquiry in terms of the written language, but his faculty with computers and working with others enabled him to put together what, for me is a brilliant dissertation" (2).

Jack referred to Boyer's work for the Carnegie Foundation (3) opening up new forms of scholarly enquiry in relation to scholarships of discovery, application, integration and teaching in his attempt to live his values more fully in his practice in his own scholarship of educational enquiry. The website http://www.actionresearch.net holds living theory theses from those engaged in self-studies of their own practice. He described how in America they found the kind of question with an "I" in it was very difficult to acknowledge that it could ever be an academic enquiry and how Jack's own practice in living educational theory gives him the feeling that "what I'm trying to do in relation to my own self studies in practice relate across art, science, dyslexia and education.

Jack then came back to the energy he had sensed at the conference and in the room, aiming to tap in to some of the pleasures that he gets out of education and describing how in the film "his face lit up in a most beautiful way a couple of times". Jack emphasized the life affirming energy that is present at such times, adding "It seems to me if we're going to have some influence in the world we've got to learn how to celebrate that energy collaboratively".

References

Adler-Collins, J. (2004) Living Action Research. See http://www.living-action-research.net/

Adler-Collins, J . (2000) A Scholarship of Enquiry'. MA Dissertation, University of Bath. Retrieved 4 July 2004 from http://www.actionresearch.net/jekan.shtml

Boyer, E. (1990). Scholarship reconsidered: Priorities of the professoriate. The Carnegie Foundation for the Advancement of Teaching: Princeton University Press. Cambridge, B. (1999)

Rayner, A. (2004) Essays and Talks on Inclusionality. Retrieved 4 July 2004 from http://www.bath.ac.uk/~bssadmr/inclusionality/

Whitehead, J. (2004) What counts as evidence in self-studies of teacher education practices? In Loughran, J. J., Hamilton, M. L., LaBoskey, V. K. & Russell, T. (2004) International Handbook of Self-study of Teaching and Teacher Education Practices. Dordrecht; Kluwer Academic Publishers.

Bernstein, B. (2000) Pedagogy, Symbolic Control and Identity. See . pp. xii-xxiv. Oxford; Rowman & Littlefield.

SECTION 3:

Dyslexic and non dyslexic writers explore creativity across science, art, dyslexia, education

Inclusional Perspectives – Making Space For Creativity in Science

An illustrated talk by Alan Rayner for 'Cascade' conference, June 2001

Most fundamentally what this talk is about, in the context of this conference, is why patterns of thought that go beyond the limitations of rationality are so very important to us, particularly as we face a growing environmental crisis of our own making.

Over 25 years ago, I painted two pictures whose meaning wasn't fully clear to me at the time.

Figure 1. 'Tropical involvement' (oil painting on board, by Alan Rayner, 1972).

This painting, made in the exuberance following the completing of my final undergraduate examinations in natural sciences, depicts the dynamic complexity of living systems. A turbulent river rushes between rock-lined banks from fiery, tiger-striped sunset towards unexpected tranquility where it allows a daffodil to emerge from its shallows. A night-bird follows the stream past intricately interwoven forest towards darkness. A dragonfly luxuriates below a fruit-laden tree, bereft of leaves. Life is wild, wet and full of surprises.

Figure 2. 'Arid Confrontation' (oil painting on board by Alan Rayner, 1973).

This painting depicts the limitations of unempathic, analytical methodology. At the end of a long pilgrimage, access to life is barred from the objective stare by the rigidity of artificial boundaries. A sun composed of semicircle and triangles is caught between Euclidean straight lines and weeps sundrops into a canalized watercourse. Moonlight, transformed into penetrating shafts of fear, encroaches across the night sky above a plain of desolation. Life is withdrawn behind closed doors.

Evidently **something** was different between the way I *experienced* and responded to life as an *involved participant*, and the way I was *analytically enquiring* about life as a *detached observer*. And this difference affected both my understanding and my feelings, as expressed in these two paintings.

I must have felt unconsciously that there was **something** about purely analytical modes of enquiry that leaves us as *observer subjects*, strangely *abstracted* from what we *observe* as *objects*. This something somehow denies the very *possibility of creative relationship*, and so is capable of inflicting profound psychological, social and environmental damage. And I believe this **something** is still very much with us all today, contributing in no small way to the conflicts and divisions that continue to afflict our human qualities of life.

But, what was this **something**? Was it an *absence* or a *presence*? Was it **something** or **nothing**? Was something missing, or was I missing something because something else, some artificially imposed, unnatural barrier was present, getting in the way of my vision?

Today I would respond to these questions by suggesting that this **something** is deeply embedded in the process of *rationalistic abstraction* through which we separate ourselves and other things from the containing space or *context* that lies both within and beyond us. This process unrealistically asserts the **presence** of *fixed boundaries* or *reference frames* to demarcate the beginnings and endings of explicit substance and actions, whilst thereby treating *space* as an **absence**, outside these boundaries and so making no contribution to the way the world and universe work. All movement is reduced to the pure kinetics of explicit, independent things whose boundaries are treated as co-extensive with their material centres.

This rationalistic *abstraction*, upon which we have become so increasingly dependent in building our science and technology, not to mention our social and political philosophy, correspondingly causes us to *exclude* from consideration everything outside our immediate focus. Consequently, we are prone to ignore context, leaving us out of touch and undernourished in an intellectual and emotional desert of our own making. We regard life and the universe like a box of Lego blocks that can be sorted, assembled and disassembled at will. This box is a fixed Euclidian reference frame, set in empty Cartesian space and absolute time, in which independent objects collide, compete and stick together, but can't **truly** *relate* because their insides are *spatially isolated* within their outsides.

It all seems such an alluringly simple and logical story – the only uncertainties lie in the randomness of independent events, but we think that statistics and risk analyses based on probability theory, itself a derivation from rationalistic logic, can help us to account for those. Moreover, this alluring simplicity fits in extremely well with our predatory and discriminatory pre-disposition to single things out from their context. Analytical left brain hemisphere at the ready, eyes facing forward on the front of our faces, giving us binocular vision and depth of field but little or no view to side or rear, we are great *sorrter-outers.* Herein lies our devotion to *quantification,* embedded in the *discreteness* of our number system and *units* of measurement as well as in *seemingly* great ideas like natural selection and genetic determinism.

But the story is a fiction, the simplicity an illusion because, as is obvious to everybody (even if many prefer to turn a blind eye to it) in reality no thing occurs in complete isolation. The discrete boundaries assumed or imposed by rational inquiry to keep things 'pure and simple', free from contaminating subjectivity and environmental noise, are artefacts. And these artefacts may actually complicate and ration our understanding by starving us of what we need to know. Real 'boundaries' are in fact dynamic interfaces, places of opportunity for reciprocal transformation between inter-communicating insides and outsides over nested scales from sub-atomic to universal. They are not fully discrete limits. Features arise dynamically, through the inductive coupling of explicit contents with their larger implicit context, which, like a hologram, can only be seen partially and in unique aspect from any one fixed viewpoint.

By the same token, we humans are as immersed in and inseparable from our living space as a whirlpool in a water flow: our every explicit action implicitly depends upon and reciprocally induces transformation of our environment. When I unfold my fingers, space-time reciprocally invaginates. Our environment becomes us as we become it – as much our inheritance as our genes. By taking self-centred action, regardless of context, we put that inheritance at risk and ultimately come intoconflict with ourselves, driven on by the rationalism that continues to underpin much purely analytical science and legalistic thinking.

This brings me to the nub of my presentation: the need for a fundamental *re-orientation* in our thinking about the *nature* of space and its *vital participation* in all *creative, evolutionary processes*, from local to global and universal scales. Indeed, I think this re-orientation can give *real meaning* to the notion of *living space* and bring us, perhaps even return us, to more empathic relationships with one another, other life forms and our surroundings. It can be brought about by combining the scientist's analytical on *explicit* actualities with the artist's imaginative vision of *implicit* **possibilities** and the dyslexic's creative *facility* for *transposition.* In other words, it is what I think this conference is fundamentally all about. By *keeping a grip* at the same time as *loosening up*, we can *make dreams real* without either *getting stuck* or *becoming unhinged.*

So, what is space? Is it something or nothing, a presence or an absence? Does it *exist?*

Herein lies, for me, the tremendous potential latent in bringing art into science and science into art: that we can appreciate the reciprocal interdependence and consequent inseparability of implicit *contextual* space and the explicit *information* that gives heterogeneous expression to that space *in the form* of features. This is the aim of the philosophy of *'inclusionality'*, currently being worked on by myself and others, whereby all things, our selves included, are viewed as dynamic contextual inclusions, no more separable from their containing space than are whirlpools from a water flow. In this view, insides are not sealed forever within the boundaries of outsides. Things are not physically discrete *bodies*, isolated by space, nor even are their outsides all interconnected by some explicit external web of material presence. Rather, they are *embodiments* of that implicit space which is not the physical absence that separates them, but rather the *labyrinth* of immaterial, non-resistive, inductive, super-conductive presence that intra-connects them by uniting their insides *through* gaps in their boundaries to their outsides.

To try to get some feel for what this means, try to imagine a world or universe with no space. Is there any *possibility* for movement or distinctiveness? Now try to imagine a world or universe of pure space. Is there *anything* there? For me, the conclusions from such imaginings are inescapable. Space is pure, implicit, insubstantial possibility, but for that possibility to be realized – expressed in distinctive, heterogeneous features – it has to be given shape, that is *in-formed,* by something explicit. Gregory Bateson alluded to this explicit something as 'the difference that makes a difference', *information.* But, by the same token, this information without contextual space is meaningless, makes no difference, has no possibility for independent expression.

Explicit information and implicit space are therefore both inseparable and dynamically co-creative. They make and are shaped by the other in the same way that the water in a river system, makes, shapes and is shaped by the space through which it flows, as it erodes rock and deposits sediment. And the making of space makes possible a flow that makes more space – an 'autocatalytic flow' - as when people walking across a meadow create and consolidate an inductive path by following their leader.

This inclusional view of information as content in relation to spatial context contrasts with the discretely packaged informational units of rationalistic, binary (either/or) logic and digital computers. Inclusional information, far from being broken up into transmissible bits and pieces of pure machine code that need to be protected from contamination by 'outside interference' or 'noise', produces vibrant, flexible *language*. It *folds* into and around the space it relates to as a dynamic matter-energy-containing boundary that nests inner spaces within outer spaces across all scales from sub-atomic to universal. This boundary is not the fixed limit of particulate things – it does not *define* – but rather provides the *mediating surface* or *interface* through which inner and outer spaces reciprocally and simultaneously transform one another.

So, the Big Story of Life and the Universe is the 'Hole Story', not the 'Whole Story'. To be dynamic, things are necessarily *in*complete: they consist of informational holes – lined spaces – not wholes and parts complete, and so static, within themselves. These holes are inductive, attractive – they have pulling power: the beauty of a cathedral is in the space that its walls line, not in these walls alone. And the holes puncture the rationalist's box that has held us like Schrödinger's Cat in secure paradoxical bondage, longing to escape into the real world where inner space connects with outer. And, as I have hinted several times, if there is anything on earth that can find these holes and show them to us for what they are, we need not look for anything rare. We need only to regard that overlooked, taken for granted *commonplace* – water, the dynamic contextual medium without which the genetic code of DNA could not be translated into the informational surface that co-creates the diversity of life itself.

I recently tried to express these thoughts in a painting entitled 'Future Present' and a painting-poem, 'The Hole in the Mole'.

Figure 3 'Future Present' (oil painting on canvas by Alan Rayner, 2000).

The gift of life lies in the creative infancy of the present, whence its message from past to future is relayed through watery channels that spill out and recombine outside the box, re-iterating and amplifying patterns over scales from microscopic to universal.

Figure 4. 'The hole in the Mole' (oil painting on canvas and poem by Alan Rayner, 2001)

I **AM** the hole

That lives in a mole

That induces the mole

To dig the hole

That moves the mole

Through the earth

That forms a hill

That becomes a mountain

That reaches to sky

That connects with stars

And brings the rain

That the mountain collects

Into streams and rivers

That moisten the earth

That grows the grass

That freshens the air

That condenses to rain

That carries the water

That brings the mole

To Life

To resume, we are not complete and separate but become our living space as it becomes us. By taking care of this space, and 'others' within it, we care for ourselves; ignore it, and we neglect and ultimately conflict with our selves. Informed by science, made imaginatively aware by art, perhaps we can learn to care more, attune to our nature and realize the true creative possibilities of human kind.

In this spirit, I'd like to end with an opening, a painting I made in the last months of 1999, entitled 'Opening Endings'.

Figure 5. 'Opening Endings' (oil painting on canvas by Alan Rayner)

An elm tree's demise, its wing-barked boundaries opened by ravages of bark beetle and fungus, makes way for new life to fill its space. Maple leaves take over the canopy between earth and sky, but their coverage is only partial, leaving openings for arriving and departing flights of woodpeckers. Fungal decay softens the wood to allow the tunnelling of long-horn beetle larvae and probing and chiselling of beak-endings. A nest cavity provides a feeding station between egg and air.

Imagination
Paper presented to Cascade conference, University of Bath, 1st July 2001.

Dr Guy Saunders, University of the West of England

Note: An overhead of Howard Hodgkin's painting Rain (1984-89) in Tate Modern collection was shown at the beginning of the presentation. The talk included video and image which are described within this paper.

The background for this paper is certainly the work I did for my PhD here at Bath that was completed in 1999. I looked at the experience of different kinds of confinement as a way of working on the use of imagination. This meant reading from the 'genre' of captivity – writings by former political prisoners and hostages – and conducting a series of interviews. The interest stemmed from training in the arts – I started a fine art degree in sculpture at St. Martin's School of Art in the 1970s. Art was the only thing I could do – at least according to the authorities at my school. It was much later, and without a direct route, that I got interested in science and particularly psychology. And this is what caused the first disjunction: why were the arts and humanities so absent from a psychology curriculum? From that, why were the so-called Two Cultures still so called? Where imagination was concerned, what was so different about artists and scientists going about their business? I could only dabble with these during that time; since then, I'm still dabbling, but the questions and issues are getting clearer. Many academics seem to baulk at the idea of a resemblance regarding what constitutes creativity. As words mean what I choose them to mean, neither more nor less, I take creativity to mean 'bringing into existence'. I use imagining to stand for both the moves we make and the moment of apprehension. So we talk about coming up with something with no idea how the coming up with something comes; this is true for artists as well as scientists. Let's have a look:

Firstly, this is Andrew Wiles, a mathematician, who spent seven years solving Fermat's Last Theorem. It isn't important what that is; I don't understand it either. Rather, listen to his comments and watch the way the scenario is put together.

Description of film clip:
> *[House exterior. Zoom in on attic window]*
> *Narrator:* Andrew abandoned his other research. He cut himself off from the rest of the world and for the next seven years he concentrated solely on his childhood passion.
> *[Interior.* Andrew Wiles at his desk in attic study room. He is writing mathematics with pen on paper]
> *Wiles [voiceover]:* I never use a computer. I sometimes might scribble. I do doodles. I start trying to find patterns really. So I'm doing calculations which try to explain

some little piece of mathematics. And I'm trying to fit it in with some previous broad conceptual understanding of some branch of mathematics. [to camera] Sometimes that will involve going and looking up in a book to see how it's done there. Sometimes it's a question of modifying things a bit. Sometimes doing a little extra calculation and sometimes you realise that nothing that's ever been done before is any use at all. You just have to find something completely new. And it's a mystery where it comes from.
[End of clip]
(Singh 1987)

Now the second clip is of Howard Hodgkin, a painter, who often spends many years working on a piece (the one I put up on the overhead at the beginning took from 1984 to 1989). Again listen to his comments.

Description of film clip:

*[**Talking heads** – Two Shot – Howard Hodgkin left screen cuts to Melvyn Bragg right screen and back]*

BRAGG: *When you're doing a painting, what do you think when you're looking at that board? Are you doing something hat you want to make this thing last?*

HODGKIN: *Yes. I'm often taking an emotion, perhaps .. My reply would be surrounded by .. Have to be very careful here. I'm wanting really to make something that will last as long as possible, but I'm trying to take a very transient emotion very often – a split second even – and turn it into something that will stay there.*

BRAGG: *Is what it starts as a sort of pulse in your mind or a picture inside your mind or a feeling inside (next utterance overlaps here)*

HODGKIN: *Oh, if only it was a picture inside my mind. No. It starts as a feeling. It starts as something and then it gradually accretes and things get stuck to it.*

BRAGG: *I find it extraordinary to try to imagine someone having a sensation, a feeling, and then turning it into painting. It is easy for people educated like I was to attempt to turn it into words, but this transferring of sensation into paint which is a process which, which .. I can understand you words 'lonely' and I can understand your words 'isolated'. I think the strain of trying to get there. You must always be feeling how do I do it?*

HODGKIN: *I'm always feeling that and of course I don't know how. And when I finish a painting I'm absolutely astonished. And that increases with age. I'm more surprised by my work now than I used to be.*

[End of clip]
(Bragg 1991)

So, *Point 1:*

We press ink to paper (key text onto a screen) in much the same way as a painter applies paint to canvas to make paintings. What is being flagged up here is the notion that texts are as much created as paintings. There are different languages, yes, but they are languages. And this is one of the problems. We treat scientific written language as if it is a ready-made allowing correspondences and representations with a real world, when, I would argue, written language is always under construction. And this is one of the problems. Being conventional is only given high status in this particular, science-reporting linguistic form. Why? Andrew Wiles has to come up with original mathematics to come up with something that will solve his theorem. Howard Hodgkin has to come up with original use of colour to come up with something in his linguistic media. It is quite conceivable to have a perfectly constructed use of English, yet have nothing to say. In neither case does it make sense to have an over-concentration on what is going on in the head of the individual. Wiles is crafting on paper or blackboard; Hodgkin on board. Neither can say how they came up with their ideas. Each has offered, because asked, an alternative linguistic account – in spoken form – which is a further and different linguistic production. The two kinds do not 'say' the same thing. We are always doing more than copying. A representation doesn't exist in the head of an individual. If only it were that easy. Nor does this entail that the process is mysterious – it may be mysterious – the idea here is to highlight that texts are not of a different status from other works. All science that is communicated is artisanship. Note: this is not saying that scientific principles aren't at play in the universe; rather, that as soon as they are articulated, they belong with all other productions that come about because of the human condition.

Point 2:

The emphasis is on usage not on outcome. We use ourselves that is what we do. The sociologist Julie Ford suggested that 'it is only because we use our bodies and brains the way we do that the world appears to us the way it does' (Ford, undated). Here usage is often about play, playing and being playful. Some people doodle, some sketch, some like the author Boris Pasternak write their diary as a way of what he described as 'limbering up' before engaging with his latest novel. [Aside: There is a paradox here of course – a creative act is always supposed to be something that has no preparation; yet everyone seems to have their ritual, superstition or, as I would prefer, what Charles Sanders Peirce referred to as Pure Play. He described it as 'a communion between self and self' with 'no rules except this very law of liberty' (Eco and Sebeok 1988: 27, 26). He hoped to educe an *'esperable uberty'* (1) – a drawing out of a hoped for fruitfulness from the play of musement. End of aside.] This is what Hodgkin refers to as a moment or feeling or sensation, transient, momentary - perhaps only a split second. Hodgkin, because he is a painter, paints – 'It's the only thing I could do.' The 'accretion' of what he does may eventually stand as a painting, in its own right, and in some way stand (in) for that moment in painterly terms.

Point 3:

There is one other insight here and that is the importance of an audience. The painting is only a painting when it is viewed, firstly it is viewed as finished by the artist and then it can continue, without the artist, to be viewed by others. Science as public domain, as crafted public work in an article or a paper, becomes an artefact that can be read or heard by others. Whether what is read or viewed is acknowledged is less important than the fact of the presence of allusions in all artefacts. Hodgkin remarks that it would be impossible to think of Rothko's work without that of Turner. He suggests that Rothko may never have seen Turner, but in some way all artists are part of the continuum of art and draw from it. Wiles remarks on the importance to his solution of the serendipitous 'casual' reading of an article that happened to be open on his desk. Dialogue or joint action or articulation (which means 'to form joint with') works because it takes place between people. The audience does not have to be present; they can be imagined. Jimmy McGovern (the writer/creator of the television programme 'Cracker') was asked what he wanted as a luxury to take to a desert island and he requested paper and pen. Why, asked the interviewer, when nobody will be able to read it? He commented that all writers write with an audience in mind even if there is no possibility of an actual audience in fact. The research I did with former hostages and political prisoners very strongly attests to this. Many writers get locked up, partly because they are writers, yet they continue to write even though they have no idea if, when or how their captivity will end. They often become their own audience becoming polyphonic rather than dissociated. Neither art, nor science nor literature is separate from society no matter what kind of isolation or confinement.

Concluding Cadenza:
It was only after looking again at *Ulysses* that I read the notes on Joyce's use of *nacheinander* and *nebeneinander.* The two German words are apparently an allusion to the work of Gotthold Lessing and give the sense of something allotropic, meaning that of two things going on simultaneously. Nacheinander translates as 'one after another' and for Lessing refers to the sense of a linear narrative prevalent in writing that uses the before, during and after construction of time. Nebeneinander means 'one next to another' and refers to the sense of construction found in painting and sculpture where aspects are juxtaposed in spatial relation to one another (Joyce 1922: 37 & 784). Both are always at play; it's just the emphases that change. Sometimes the juxtapositioning creates surprises.

Magritte was preoccupied by the taken-for-granted real. He made a series of paintings designed to sabotage our sense of the familiar. The painting L'Usage de Parole 1 (The Use of Words 1) is well known and highlights the problem of the really real and the conventionally real. The realist image of the pipe, painted using all the tricks that fool the eye into seeing a three dimensional image, is placed with the painted words 'This is not a pipe'. We would expect the word 'Pipe' to be written, just as learning cards are used in schools that show a picture of an apple and the word 'apple'. In overthrowing our sense of the familiar, Magritte drew attention to the way conventions in painting make the work appear as it does. The idea of a faithful copy is disputed; art became an exercise not in copying the world but rather in constructing it. By making our seeing habits obvious, classically seen world is imagined and how it could be imagined differently.

Apprehension seems to require collapsing this paradox or ambiguity; improvisation, imagination, creativity seem to call for being moved and not blocking the movement.

As Einstein, a dyslexic I believe, said, 'Imagination is more important than knowledge. For knowledge is limited, whereas imagination embraces the entire world ...'.

References:

Bragg, Melvyn (1991) Howard Hodgkin. *The South Bank Show.* LWT.

Eco, Umberto and Sebeok, Thomas A. (editors) (1988) *The Sign of Three: Dupin, Holmes, Peirce.* Bloomington and Indianapolis: Indiana University Press.

Ford, J (Undated) *Developing Research,* Middlesex University: Course Book for Postgraduate Diploma in Research Methods in the Social Sciences.

Hodgkin, Howard (1984-89) *Rain.* Tate Modern.

Joyce, James (1922/1993) *Ulysses.* Oxford: Oxford University Press.

Renee Magritte, L'Usage de Parole 1 (The Use of Words 1) 1928-29, William N. Copley, New York.

Singh, Simon (1987) Fermat's Last Theorem. BBC.

Towards a Rapprochement between Artists and Educators

Ketaki Kushari Dyson

I am delighted that I have been asked to contribute a short piece on my play *Night's Sunlight* to this collection of papers. Written originally in Bengali in 1990, this play was premièred at Manchester City of Drama 1994 by a visiting theatre group from Calcutta, with a 'simultaneous interpretation' in English relayed through headphones to those who wanted it. In 1997 I made a proper translation of the play into English, and in 2000 this English version was produced under the auspices of the British Centre for Literary Translation at the University of East Anglia as a Millennium Festival project, with an Arts Council grant from lottery money. Considering the constraints presented by a small budget, a long and complex cross-cultural play, and limited rehearsal time, it was a splendid and spirited production, directed by Gail Rosier of Henley-on-Thames. The English production itself was cross-cultural, as a white cast acted the Bengali roles. Bath was not one of the cities and towns we were able to visit in 2000, and I regretted this, as I had a friend there who had shown interest in the idea.

That friend was Morag Kiziewicz, who already knew me as a poet and translator. After the play's Millennium tour was over, we met again at a poetry festival, where she bought the English version of the play. Morag was the prime mover in bringing *Night's Sunlight* to the Cascade Conference at Bath University in the summer of 2001.

The presentation at this conference was a 'rehearsed reading', with lighting, props, music, and costumes as in the original production, with as much physical movement as possible, but allowing the cast to retain their scripts, inasmuch as actors cannot remember the lines of a long play after a gap. To re-memorize their lines, they would have needed a longer period of rehearsal, which would have needed more funding. We had trepidations as to how it would go, but as it turned out, it went very well. The only pity was that more conference delegates did not turn up at the performance – why didn't they? – and that it being outside of term-time, the students of Bath University were absent.

Morag told me that the 'rehearsed reading' mode was in a way more interesting for the conference because it was more educative: it revealed the 'internal works' of the performing process, making it abundantly clear how much effort actors actually have to pack into the enactment of a lengthy word-rich dramatic work. For a full performance they have to learn their lines *and* their gestures, expressions, movements, and work together as a team, inclusive of the music and lighting assistants. Actors usually have to work for a pittance, and very few can make a proper living out of acting in serious plays. All the more reason why, when they are making a heroic effort on the

stage to make things come alive, they deserve the rewarding presence of more viewers. Those in the paid employment of institutions could perhaps show an awareness of this?

The attempt to make one of my Bengali works accessible in the country where I have made my permanent home since the sixties, and of which I am a fully paid up citizen, was the outcome of an urge which I believe is natural to creative artists. When we create a work of art, we want to share it with others. The creation itself is not a solipsistic act. I may be sitting alone, pen in hand, or fingers poised over a tap-tapping typewriter, or facing a computer screen, but what I write will be shaped as much by me as by a host of other agents, visible and invisible. I am myself a child of the world I inhabit, but not a passive child, for to some extent I create my world too. For instance, in my case, the moment I decided that I would carry on some of my writing in Bengali even though I was settling in England, I created a special world for myself, in which, in addition to everything else all writers must do to keep developing, I had to maintain extra filaments of connections and communications across thousands of miles in order to remain a publishable and published writer in my mother tongue. I have to keep pace with my language's changes, for nothing stays still. The social and cultural universe of the language is evolving all the time. I am myself contributing to those changes by my own writings. I have to maintain contact with distant audiences, be able to say something meaningful to them, bring to them some of my experiences garnered in this country. All this is in addition to persuading native English-speakers that I could be an interesting writer, that given suitable opportunities, I could make a contribution to the cultural life of this country too. This process usually involves overcoming prejudices, because generally speaking, over here writing in an Asian language tends to lower an author's status, even if that person also writes in English.[1]

The product which I call my work – in either of my two writing languages – and over which I strive to exercise copyright, comes into being as an offspring of myself and my world with all its dazzling complexities and maddening inconsistencies, as a result of the dynamic interaction between the two. My daily Western world goes into my Bengali writing, and my 'submerged' Indian world swims into my English writing. Having conjured this new thing up, on which I fancy I have stamped a seal of myself, I immediately long to share it with others, to give it back to where it really belongs: the world which had played its own part in this generative act.

It is an urge to extend the frontiers of a limited self, and can probably be subsumed under a broad band of spiritual urges which prompt us to confront our mortality and do what we can to balance it. We create children; we make peace with this world, which brought us forth and will reclaim us in death, or with the concept of a deity. 'Give beauty back, beauty, beauty, beauty, back to God, beauty's self and beauty's giver' – wrote an English poet, Gerard Manley Hopkins in 1882.[2] In 1937, a Bengali poet, Rabindranath Tagore, wrote lines to his past which I have myself translated thus:

> Companion at my back, tear the bindings of dreams;
> and those treasures of suffering, tinted futilities of desires,
> which you have snatched and guarded from death's grasp –
> give them back to death.[3]

Earlier in his career, in 1892, Tagore had written a wonderful poem set in riverine East Bengal, which has become a classic in Bengali. In it a golden harvest of rice, stacked up on the brink of a rain-swollen river, is carried away by a mysterious stranger who comes singing a song, sailing in a boat, which has room for the rice but not for the peasant who had produced it. A kaleidoscope of interpretations has been bestowed on the poem; my favourite is the one that sees the story as a metaphor for an artist's fate. In some ways an artist is like such a tiller of the soil, who offers his work, produced in conjunction with nature, to an unknown recipient, knowing that this way at least his work will be safe, though he himself will perish. Standing, as it were, on the edge of a monsoon-swollen oceanic river, we artists scan the horizon for the appearance of mysterious, ambiguous strangers who might be persuaded to take our harvest on board, even though we ourselves might be left stranded on an unsteady ground, surrounded by swirling waters.[4]

Well, it is especially lonely to be an author in diaspora, not knowing how to share one's work with the immediate community in which one's lot is cast, uncertain of the welcome one will receive. The recent successes of Indian authors in this country have been mainly in the field of the novel, and only for those writing in English. The 'Indian English novel' has been made into something of a cult genre, disjointed from the rest of contemporary writing in the Indian languages, given an identity and claimed on behalf of Western readers by the media and the academia, and packaged as a saleable commodity by the West's publishing industry. Poets and dramatists of Indian origin, even if writing in English, have not been brought into the British mainstream in the same way. And generating intelligent interest in Indian-language writing remains a difficult task, notwithstanding the slight advances in multiculturalism that have taken place in very recent years. The reluctance of people to take seriously a play translated from Bengali was quite noticeable. Wherever we went, we had small audiences only, and schools were regrettably the worst in persuading pupils and teachers to attend. As all our shows had to be one-off events in the venues concerned, there was no way we could lure the absentees back to the next show, as it were.

One of my main aims in translating *Night's Sunlight* into English was to show that this play set in a British Bengali living-room was born of twin cultural matrices and could be claimed as much by speakers of English as by speakers of Bengali. Those who were persuaded that it could be interesting in spite of its origins in another language, or *especially interesting* because of it, did, I think, see my point. Because the immediate setting was familiar enough, and yet the language in which the vision originated was different, they could view the world through a somewhat different window, and found it rewarding. Reviews and other feedback which we pasted on the play's website testify to that. Released into English, the play could touch speakers of other languages too: amongst them were individuals with roots in Slovakia, Hungary, Iran, Pakistan, Brazil, Germany, and Belgium. They all felt that the play had pertinent messages for us and our times, across national frontiers.

In our times of mass culture, artists are facing an uphill struggle in fulfilling their roles as educators. I myself believe that artists do have a role to play in society as educators and am always looking for opportunities to break down the barriers between the academic/pedagogic and artistic/creative domains. In the first half of the twentieth century a poet like Rabindranath Tagore could found his own school, university, and institute of rural reconstruction to fulfil his dreams in this respect, and his example inspired Leonard Elmhirst's experiments at Dartington. As the twentieth century progressed, however, the scenario changed substantially. The concept of authorship was declared untrustworthy if not outright dead. Unwilling to grant status to creative writers, critics dug trenches where they carried on their post-mortem of works of art. With this 'trahison des clercs', the business of culture became an adjunct to a vast, globalized entertainment industry serviced by modern technology. Serious drama fell into the same predicament as poetry, because it could not be readily converted into market-driven mass entertainment.

Pick up any theatre brochure and start to scan its pages. You will soon find that the buzz-word in theatrical publicity is 'funny'. It is as if every play must be sold as 'funny', or it will not sell at all. One of these days I may chance upon a brochure which advertises *King Lear* or *Oedipus Rex* as 'funny' too.

Certain sectors of the commercial film and television industry have cast their long shadows on the entire world of dramatic art. Audiences fed continuously on sit-coms, soaps, and movies portraying violent crimes and scenes of war and torture, policemen and detectives, robbers and gangsters, soon lose their ability to appreciate the nuances of serious drama. And now that Bollywood is extending its long arms to this country, in future any drama that pretends to have Indian roots may be expected to show some family resemblance to entertainment stemming from

that gigantic industry! A play like *Night's Sunlight* came into being because its first birth was in Bengali, and it could be staged by actors from Calcutta's non-commercial 'group theatre' movement, who keep experimental theatre alive. It could later happen in English because the Director of a key institution like the British Centre for Literary Translation took an interest in the translated text and was able to obtain Arts Council funding for its production. It is this chain of events which opened for it the possibility of becoming an educational tool in this country.

If we wish to steer ourselves away from the highway where culture is an adjunct of commerce, those who believe in the educative value of art have to come together. I believe we could shape things better with more adroit co-operation. It is individuals with vision who can kick-start new cultural and pedagogic processes. Night's Sunlight is already being taught at the University of Wales Swansea, where the English production had been premièred in the campus theatre as a part of the Writing Diasporas Conference. The play had such an impact on one teacher from the English Department, Ann Heilmann, that she sat up all night incorporating it into a course on 'post-colonial feminist' writers which she taught. In November 2002 I went to meet the students who were studying it that year, and met others too, teachers and research students. I was given a warm welcome. I talked about my background, my other work, my struggles as a diasporic writer, why I translated the play. I read some of my poetry. I answered questions. It was a valuable exchange of ideas. One student who had studied the play in 2000 and is now doing her MA at Cardiff came to Swansea to hear me. A research student of Mexican-American origin claims to have become my fan and has sent a copy of the play to her mother.

So this is a cascading effect springing from a) the original decision of the Director of the British Centre for Literary Translation to push for the production of the translated play, b) the decision of the convenors of the Writing Diasporas Conference to stage the play at the campus theatre in Swansea, and c) the subsequent decision of one individual in the English Department there to go ahead and teach the text. Guided by a discerning teacher, thanks to her infectious enthusiasm, students had come to appreciate the slightly different cultural provenance of the text and had become receptive to my other work. Suddenly I had come alive to them as a real contemporary author living and working in Britain. I was no longer a marginal and muted figure: they could hear my voice!

The interest and active participation of the teacher is a crucial factor. If a few more teachers were to adopt the play in courses they taught, the news about the existence of such a play might spread, the interest generated by the play could then be used as an entry-point to introduce some of my other work, and thus I might be able to reach a wider audience in this country. That would lessen my sense of isolation in Britain. I might begin to feel that after all these years I did have a community in Britain to which I belonged!

As is evident from the events outlined above, certain academics are helping: without their help I would not have even got to this point. I was interviewed by another academic, Gabriele Griffin – now at Hull University – who saw the play at Swansea, and a reference to it may turn up in her next book! There is already a reaction amongst teachers against the trends that consigned authors to the rubbish heap. Some of them are interested in making the teaching of literature lively and down-to-earth once more, freed from the burden of excessive jargon. The task now is to build on these new beginnings.

As those who have copies of *Night's Sunlight* know, I wrote a long Preface to it, calling it the Translator's Prologue, in which I covered, amongst other things, issues such as diasporic authorship, bilingual writing, the role of translation as a tool of inter-cultural communication, the comparative receptions of Indian writing in English and of Indian writing translated from the indigenous Indian languages, the quarrel between those who value drama as literature and those who value it only as performance. The few who have read this Preface swear by it and say that it should be compulsory reading for all academics teaching 'post-colonial literature'. I would say an 'Amen' to that, but when one is outside institutions, it is hard work persuading people within them, so I need more allies from within the citadels!

The rich irony in all this is that I was trained for an academic career myself, but discrimination on grounds of race, gender, and marital status in the Britain of the sixties, seventies, and eighties saw to it that I could not put my foot in the door. If I was within the edifice, as it were, I could have worked towards the rapprochement of art and education from within, but as things are, I must struggle valiantly from without!

The Cascade performance enabled me to reach a new set of people. Those who watched it witnessed the power that words can have on the stage. This power can be harnessed for education. A handful of people at Bath University appreciated the play's educational potential at once. Alan Rayner saw in it the spirit of 'Inclusionality' and brought me into his e-mail sharing-circle. He has been keen that the play should be adopted as a teaching text and has commented on the importance of its messages in the current world. Jack Whitehead recommended a production which could lead to the making of a DVD, which would enhance the play's value as an educational tool and widen its audience. We still have copies of the play-text that were printed to accompany the Millennium production, but our limited funding did not enable us to make a high-quality video recording. It would be a boon to redress this so that the text and a DVD could together become a compact teaching kit for classrooms and workshops.

This is a play in which ideas are important, a play to make people sit up and think. Many core issues of our times are aired and thrashed in it. It asks us to see that there are no hard boundaries between our Self and the Other. The scope of inter-disciplinary discussion around the play is substantial. In 2000 our best workshop was at the Institute of Social and Cultural Anthropology, Oxford. A few friends who have not seen a performance, but have only read the play, have noted its power as a text. Among them is the poet and critic Anne Stevenson. To read a play-text and see it in the head requires some training: in the past we used to be trained to do that in our literature courses. A sterile quarrel between 'page and stage' has set in since those days. A word-rich play is automatically literature, but when enacted on the stage, with all the razzle-dazzle of theatre, the discourses release passionate, powerful energies which audiences can take home with them and which can feed their thoughts and emotions. This is what does happen when people see my play. I have been assured by quite a few people that watching it has been a transformative and educative experience for them. They have gone home and talked late into the night about the issues raised by it.

I therefore hope that working through education, it might be possible to bring this play to the attention of a wider audience. The play was actually given a very positive review in the journal *Writing In Education*, but there has been no query in the nature of a follow-up from that, because, I suspect, where so many people are chasing their dreams, an individual has to take a personal interest for anything to happen. A DVD would undoubtedly be an asset in a teaching situation, and – if a project to make it – in the spirit of a partnership between art and education – could indeed come about. I would be thrilled.

[1] See my paper 'Forging a Bilingual Identity: A Writer's Testimony', in Burton, Ardener, and Dyson, editors, *Bilingual Women: Anthropological Approaches to Second-Language Use*, Berg, Oxford and Providence, 1994.

[2] Hopkins, 'The Leaden Echo and the Golden Echo', quoted from *Poems and Prose of Gerard Manley Hopkins*, ed. by W. H. Gardner, Penguin Books, Harmondsworth, Middlesex, 1961 reprint.

[3] Quoted from *I Won't Let You Go: Selected Poems* of Rabindranath Tagore, translated by Dyson, Bloodaxe Books, Newcastle upon Tyne, 1991.

[4] An English version of this poem, 'The Golden Boat', may be found in the *Selected Poems* of Rabindranath Tagore, translated by William Radice, Penguin Books, Harmondsworth, Middlesex, 1985.

Poetry, Language, Dyslexia

Morag Kiziewicz

Introduction

This chapter draws on the workshop of the same title that was held at the Cascade conference and suggests that we may be doing dyslexic people an injustice by focusing on dyslexic difficulties rather than strengths. Dyslexia is often seen as primarily an issue of having a difficulty with words.   Is "difficulty with words" (the meaning of the word "dys-lexia") an accurate description for dyslexia? Many dyslexic people are highly able verbally. Although it may take a dyslexic person a long time to reply to a question the answer will often be comprehensive and insightful, and they may come up with remarkable spoken summation that if asked they are unable to instantly recall or repeat.

Dyslexic children in schools often self select or are guided away from subject areas that are primarily of a written and reading focus. This is due to the perceived difficulty with words and the feedback they receive on their written work, and the result is dyslexic career choices that do not reflect the individual's true nature and ability. Our education system, even our computer spell and grammar checkers, in being predicated on spelling and linear structures, are marginalizing the true literacy and poetry of our language and of our dyslexic students.

In 2001 a group of winners in a National Poetry competition were announced, and it was subsequently discovered that all of them were dyslexic. Could this be an accident, coincidence or possibly even related to a specific dyslexic ability with words?   If so, what is the nature of this ability and how can we ensure we foster creative writing skills in the same way that we seek to foster other abilities?

Poetry and Dyslexia

The relationship between dyslexia and poetry is relatively well documented. Among the best known dyslexic poets W.B.Yeats stands tall. William Butler Yeats (1865 - 1939) described being "banished by the world and banishing the world". His poem "Among School-children" written with himself in the role of elderly Irish School inspector, is an indictment on the school system of the day and enlighteningly suggestive of the dyslexic school experience as described by
so many dyslexic adults now

"I dream of a Ledaen body, bent
Above a sinking fire. A tale that she
Told of a harsh reproof, or trivial event
That changed some childish day to tragedy - ".

"W.B Yeats is a world-renowned poet. He wrote many famous poems such as 'Among School-children' and' No Second Try'. He also won the Nobel Prize in poetry. He is highly respected among the poets of today. He is world famous in all eyes. However, Yeats was actually dyslexic. When he was a child, he did so poorly in school that his father decided to teach him at home." (Good Schools Guide). Perhaps his father's choice is what enabled William Butler to rise above the difficulties he encountered and to find words to describe the indistinguishable boundaries associated with joy at the end of the same poem:

Labour is blossoming or dancing where
The body is not bruised to pleasure soul.
Nor beauty born out of its own despair,
Nor blear-eyed wisdom out of midnight oil
O Chestnut tree great rooted blossomer,
Are you the leaf, the blossom or the bole?
O body swayed to music, O brightening glance
How can we know the dancer from the dance?

Critics describe the period that Yeats was writing in as one of transformation, Arnold Toynbee talks of poetry addressing "the schism in the soul". Yeats, founder member of "the Rhyming Club" said he aimed to "articulate emotion which had no relation to any public intent".

In the poem, Lapis Lazuli, he associates war with negative cynicism and identifies the need to have a positive approach to life with the resulting ability to recover and take the long view. He describes the decimation of cultures and in this poem he engages with the image carved in lapis lazuli by a chinese craftsman from an ancient civilisation. In the final stanza he takes us into the carving and beyond to the mountain view where it was made and brings the characters to life, we can feel we are moving through the space time boundaries into a continuum, a time shift.

Every discoloration of the storm,
Every accidental crack or dent,
Seems a water course or an avalanche
Or lofty slope where it still snows
Though doubtless plum or cherry-branch
Sweetens the little half-way house
There three men climb towards, and I
Delight to imagine them seated there,

There, on the mountain and the sky
On all the tragic scenes they stare
One asks for   mournful melodies
Accomplished fingers begin to play.
Their eyes mind many worlds, their eyes,
Their ancient, glittering eyes, are gay.

Son of a painter and poet, home educated after his difficult school experiences, W.B. clearly had the kind of visual mind and holistic imagination that we tend to expect from dyslexic people and in his poems there seems to be no difficulty with words.

Spoken versus written language

The debate between the spoken and written language is older even than Plato and Socrates, yet it is curiously pertinent to our understanding of dyslexia today. This dyslexic ability with words in poetry describes an undertow, yet the written structure that achieves this is one that would probably be covered in red and green lines in a computer grammar check or by the marking of a handwritten essay. The structure of writing words in our expected styles, such as an essay, appears to be a linear aptitude. However this only describes the ABC of spelling and not the whole richness of vocabulary and literature that Yeats and Shakespeare display and that is evident in story telling rather than reading. The way we hear sound, rhythm and cadence is vital. Poetry only comes truly alive when it is spoken, for example throughout W.S.Graham's The Nightfishing the sound and rhythm are hypnotic and we can hear the gulls, the waves, the bell, and sense the movement of the sea and the impact on the mind. In stanza **7** for example:

Far out, faintly rocked,
Struck the sea bell.

Home becomes this place,
A bitter night, ill
To labour at dead of.
Within all the dead of
All my life I hear
My name spoken out
On the break of the surf.
I, in Time's grace,
The grace of change, am
Cast into memory.
What a restless grace
To trace stillness on.

The deeper rhythms and layers and elements of the poem become both clearer and more profound when the rhythm of the poem is heard rather than read, and the flow of the stanzas describe the elements of the changing sea and emotions,

> *O my love, keep the day*
> *Leaned at rest, leaned at rest.*
>
> *What one place remains*
> *Home as darkness quickens?*

Language structure and neurology

Holistic vision and strange or unusual juxtaposition of words are acceptable in written poetry if not in grammar, and often bring a third dimension to the meaning. The structure of language can be linear or holistic, however we do not teach the holistic aspects, preferring to concentrate on spelling, grammar and 'literacy' in the most linear meaning of the tem. Melanie Phillips took a teacher to task in her book 'All Must Have Prizes', describing in very negative terms how the teacher had marked a child correct for writing 'medfords' and 'smiles' when the correct answer was metaphors and similes. The accuracy of this assessment depends on the assessment criteria, if the criteria was solely spelling, then yes this answer was incorrect. However if the criteria was understanding, then clearly the child understood the answer to which the question referred and to mark her wrong in such a case is "a harsh reproof" and does not improve the child's understanding - she will not know where she went "wrong".

The development of the English language has many of its roots in Latin. It is interesting to note the root of the word right, comes from the Sanskrit 'rta' meaning whole, complete. This was generally been taken to refer to the right hand, however given our contemporary understanding of neurology we can now understand rta, right to mean right brain, whole. Complete.
Right brain, left hand is a fluid holistic three dimensional understanding, and many dyslexic people are right brain dominant. There is a traditional fear of the left with its apparent chaos, random, serendipitous connections, "my right hand doesn't know what my left is doing". This is a fear of the breaking down of barriers, control mechanisms, and boundaries, and is interestingly applied to the left hand (right brain holistic abilities) rather than to the right hand (left brain linear function). We understood that the left brain gave us strengths such as organizational, linear and martial skills which led to global dominance. We have relatively recently allowed people to write with their left hand, and this is still sometimes regarded with suspicion, one (erroneous) study even suggesting that left handed people die younger! Many dyslexic people, but by no means all, are left handed.

We seek control and the ordered structure that the left brain and right hand give us. We call this objective, although all our so-called "objective" discourse is informed by the subjective and by our lived experience. In so doing we lose an escape route for the inner quiet unheard voice. Rage, and joy, fear and love are expressed through poetry, the subjective is heard through poetry, but not usually in academic writing. This is why dyslexic people find academic writing such a trial.

The objective outer voice was until recently the only voice heard in academic writing, for example my Masters Degree required that any sentence with "I" in it be changed to the objective by using instead the term "one". Academic writing requires an organised structure : a beginning, a middle, an end. Compare this to poetry, starting in the middle, going who knows where, looping back on itself. Strange punctuation too, line breaks, commas in unexpected places, drawing breath.

Andrew Shelley's review of John James' A Tongue Not Distanced From the
Feeling Brain describes this:

> "James' language is such a skin or sail that both resists yet gives in order to steer a course, draw a line, that of the 'level trace'. This may be true of all poetic language, yet it is especially true of James' 'wet skin' 'skin as damp as steam'.

Perhaps now we are beginning to understand the essential aspects of emotional intelligence and the importance of the subjective in the lived experience, we will begin to encourage the holistic to flourish once more.

Living Language and Whole Writing

Language is live and vibrant and changing all the time. Mobile phone technology has changed our "text language" and there have been poetry competitions in this abbreviated word form. There is evidence for new languages in computer speak:

> "I also used speak fluent Z80, 68000 and x86 assembly, but I've been out of practise for a while. I got out of x86 before I learned about GDTs and LDTs and that sort of stuff - I come from the era of fitting it all into a 64K block and LIKING it that way".

> "There is no "Word version" of these texts. Really. You can grab the HTML version and load it into Word if you want the fancy-shmancy headers, but it's exactly the same content." Waider

Charles Bernstein suggests:

> "The reinvention, the making of a poetry for our time, is the only thing that makes poetry matter. And that means, literally, making poetry matter, that is making poetry that intensifies the matter or materiality of poetry—acoustic, visual, syntactic, semantic. Poetry is very much alive when it finds ways of doing things in a media-saturated environment that only poetry can do, but very much dead when it just retreads the same old same old."

Editing of dyslexic work becomes a process of knitting, a continuum of threads. How every dyslexic hates the editor or learning support tutor who in making suggestions for restructuring their writing appears to "attack" their garment, a thread pulled here a word cut there and the whole thing unravels before their eyes! Dyslexic people often enjoy the physicality of writing and will have many drafts which are written on and pasted up and physically sculpted before reaching the final work.

There is academic discussion in Higher Education, particularly in the art world regarding alternative format to written material, particularly the dissertation, to give access to dyslexic and disabled people. And projects exploring ways of assessment, such as choice for several assessment methods.

There is certainly hope that in the future we will embrace dyslexic literacy skills by avoiding making too quick assumptions about the nature of "difficulty with words". There is also concern that while most of the research and intervention currently still focuses on how to make right brain dominant dyslexic people fit a left brain world. There is the potential that we will lose the abilities that being right brain dominant can bring unless a true social model of disability is applied for dyslexia, particularly within the literacy curriculum.

Biography

Bernstein, Charles
http://www.press.uchicago.edu/Misc/Chicago/044106.html

Catling, B. (1990) The Stumbling Block, its INDEX, Book Works, London Limited Edition

Graham, W.S. (1996) Selected Poems, Faber and Faber.

Phillips, M. (1996/97) All Must Have Prizes, Time Warner.

Yeats, W.B., The Collected Poems, Wordsworth Editions Ltd.
http://www.geocities.com/Athens/5379/yeats_index.html

Andrew Shelley's review of John James' A Tongue Not Distanced From the
Feeling Brain in Tears in the Fence, Editor David Caddy, Stourpaine, Blandford Forum, Dorset
DT11 8TN

Art, Dyslexia and Creativity

Dr Iain Biggs

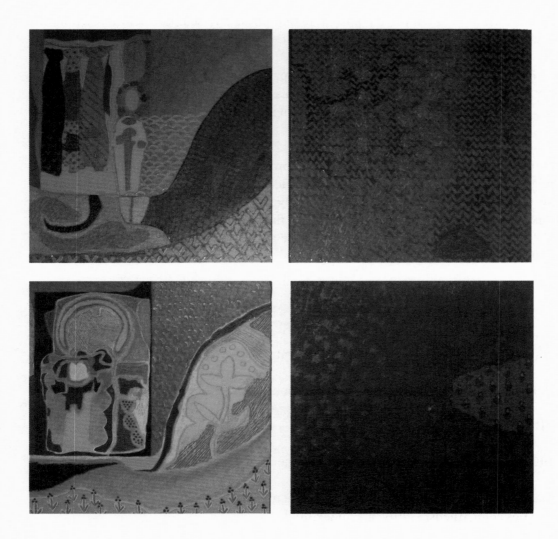

Twelve years ago, in the middle of a tutorial, I was diagnosed as dyslexic by one of my own students. I didn't believe her but she was the dyslexic mother of a dyslexic daughter who she had just coached into University so, by the time she'd finished talking to me, I did believe her. Probably the most significant outcome of that conversation is that as an academic I stopped feeling like an illegal immigrant on a fake passport and began simply to feel like another of the resident aliens. This is not a laughing matter. I think it's difficult for people who are comfortable in the academic culture to understand just how repressive the shadow of academia can be and it's is one of the things I want to talk about.

As a child I wanted to be a poet. I could improvise and tell stories for hours on end. Unfortunately I couldn't spell, but I could draw, so like an awful lot of dyslexics before and after me, I got shunted off to the art world and a long time later I ended up as a principal lecturer running a Fine Art degree course. This is the first time I have been asked to speak about my discipline as a private individual and I think this personal background has a bearing on what I am going to say. I want to talk about the essential cultural ambiguity that should stay with us when we talk about art, creativity, and dyslexia. For painters ambiguity is one of those things we have to live with. What I have to say here is a very personal point of view.

There are now good bodies of well-researched evidence that tell us that there are links between visual spatial ability associated with dyslexia and the forms of thinking that aid creative work in the arts. It has even become possible to identify differences in orientation between what is called design minds and sign minds through the work of Dr Beverly Steffert. This is very important in the struggle to get dyslexia taken seriously in the education world and the last thing I would want is to detract from that important task. However it is vital that we keep asking questions about the connections between dyslexia, creativity, and art.

About 1993 I heard an argument for art schools as specialist education centers for dyslexia put forward by the artist Susan Hiller, and Professor Gosling hints at something similar in his paper. I would want to resist any move in that direction. The reason is complicated but has to do with the fact that I would be very concerned if we were to isolate the type of creative thinking associated with dyslexia, to put it in a special educational context. I think that would fix a set of relationships that we need to see as fluid and changing. I would argue that we should be very wary of arguments that claim that there is a clear-cut link between art, dyslexia and creativity and that the link is always positive. This view stems from my belief that, firstly, imagination is prior to and more important than any single area of human activity and development and, even more important, than art.

Secondly, we should never take for granted that creativity is a positive human attribute. Torturers, I am told, are often highly creative people.

Thirdly if we slip into assuming that dyslexics have some innate tendency to be visually artistic this may turn out to be another way of ignoring their real potential as, say, archaeologists, poets, or computer scientists. These beliefs run parallel to my sense that what creativity and the arts and the thinking of dyslexics may have in common is the potential to work imaginatively between and across categories. However that potential can only be realised if we have an appropriate model of the imagination.

The realization of our creative potential always depends on how we understand and use our creativity. Creativity has no innate value in itself and is a highly ambiguous attribute. Imagination is more fundamental than what we call creativity. The imagination's ability to dissolve the rigidity of categories by working between and across them is vitally important because of the paradoxical nature of categories. On the one hand, categories give vital structure and help us make sense of the flood of our experience. On the other hand they constantly threaten to fix our understanding, to blind us to the fluidity of that experience. I happen to believe that the imagination is one of those fundamental tools by which we negotiate and work with the paradox of categories. Art is of course only one version of that tool, although I would argue an extremely important one.

Thinking about the relationship between art, dyslexia and creativity is made more complex both by their ambiguous values and their constantly changing relationship to the wider social context. When I was a student I thought imagination and innovation were more or less synonymous and took it for granted they were both of equal value. In this respect I was a product of a particular type of art education. Only when I tried to understand changes in both art and society did I see that imaginative creation requires adaptation based on an understanding of existing models and traditions as well as the ability to extend, modify, or exceed those models or traditions. Today I see innovation as one of three fundamental aspects of imaginative work, but only one.

I would also want to question the art world's current obsession with innovation, particularly given the fact that it is very closely linked to an obsession with novelty and the function that novelty plays in our consumer culture. This is why I want to keep in question how we link art, creativity, dyslexia and imagination. Another reason is that the best contemporary thinking on imagination that I know stresses the importance of our imaginative relationship to what remains potent in the past. It even argues that imaginative re-interpretation or re-evaluation of the past now may be more critical to our survival than innovation. Historically this reverses the priorities of many modern assumptions about imagination and creativity. However, while ecologists might find this more conservationist view persuasive, students with dyslexia or other artists may well find this harder to accept, largely because they are conditioned to identify creativity with innovation.

One consequence is that if we encourage dyslexics to see themselves as artistic or creative rather than people capable of being imaginative in the broader sense, we may devalue the real potential of their visual spatial imagination. Creativity is an instinct without any intrinsic value. To evaluate any creative act, for example what is called 'creative accounting', we need to locate creativity in a wider context. If we accept that dyslexics have a propensity to higher than average creativity we still need to keep asking in what context is that creativity used?
I know of two specific locations where the incidence of dyslexia is higher than average. One is in art and design education. The other is in the prison population. I would want to argue that where dyslexics end up depends on whether they are helped by their education to find opportunities to develop as imaginative people, not just creative people. Years of working with art students confirms my sense that many dyslexics arrive on art and design courses because these offer the only form of Higher Education they can access. The students certainly have some visual talent, but first and foremost they are bright survivors of the secondary education system who miraculously are still hungry to learn. Some of them can benefit from art education, others leave angry and resentful. In my view there are far too many frustrated former art students in the world hooked on a very limited notion of creativity and trapped by their self identification as artists. There are also, I suspect, far too few imaginative educated dyslexics are at the cutting edge of other disciplines and professions.

The case of Tracey Emin, probably the best known dyslexic artist in Britain today, may help to illustrate why I think we need to keep asking questions about how and why we link art, creativity and dyslexia. As a dyslexic and famous contemporary artist, Emin might appear to reinforce the idea that the visual spatial abilities of the design mind are central to success. However to establish that point we would need to be sure that her success is due to her outstanding spatial ability. Or is it due to a reversal of the gender role, where once it was only male artists that were able to cash in on the role of a bohemian lifestyle? Just what are the real relationships between her success and dyslexia. This is a question worth asking.

My point is that being a successful artist in today's overcrowded and media driven art world can involve many different types of creativity. The function and nature of art has been undergoing regular and radical changes for well over 100 years and continues to do so. Is visual spatial ability equally relevant to all art manifestations? If not where does that leave the dyslexics who have been told "being a dyslexic may be hell, but at least you are going to be good at art."

I implied earlier that the potential ability of the design mind to work imaginatively with the paradox of categories might be its most fundamental value. If we work in education and also happen to be concerned with imagination or dyslexia, it is vital that we keep alive commitment to the variety of ways in which people make sense of the world. In this context for institutions to require art, creativity, or dyslexia to make sense only in terms of dominant or fashionable categories is always to diminish the potential for both the individuals and society.

Education needs to keep in mind the philosopher Geraldine Finn's observation:
"We are always both more and less than the categories which name and divide us", and there have been times when some of the things that have been said about myself as an object of study by those who study dyslexia have made me feel profoundly angry. However difficult and demanding the implication of what Geraldine Finn has to say may be, I think this observation is central because when we take for granted fixed categories, including those of art, dyslexia, and creativity, we start to deny the fluidity of our lived experience. If, as one contemporary philosopher has suggested, the future of Europe depends on our imagination, we have all the more reason to take Finn's observation to heart.

Reinforcing the importance of Imagination from another perspective, Barbara Stafford argues that "the imagination itself is analogous to biology in that its evolution requires the unpredictable generation of a rich diversity of alternatives and conjectures". Diversity means in the arts dissolving the current fixation that creativity has to do with exclusively on what is new, what is coming next. The work of the German artist Anselm Kiefer is an excellent example of an imagination oriented by re-thinking the past. He is to my knowledge the only contemporary artist cited by a philosopher, an eminent historian and an eminent psychologist as making a genuine contribution to our understanding of the world.

Having stressed the importance of imagination and fluidity in education I want to briefly comment on the findings of a report written by the Advisory Committee on Creative Culture in Education.

Their view is that creativity is possible in all areas of human activity and that all people are creative while demonstrating their creative ability differently. If so, why all this fuss about art? They also claim when individuals find their strengths this can have an enormous effect on their self esteem and overall achievement. I would agree absolutely, while remembering that as a schoolboy my finding creative ways to steal cigarettes for my classmates did far more for my battered self-esteem as an undiagnosed dyslexic than anything anyone said to me about my art work. When they argue that creativity is imagination fashioned to produce activity of originality and value I obviously can't fault them, but I still worry that they are side stepping the question of who is going to define originality and value.

At present there are two institutional answers to that question. One answer is the National Curriculum that in practice tends to see creativity as something that happens in the arts rather than as a core element in all good teaching. The second answer is within the art world that becomes ever more entangled with media so that provocative, media-friendly novelty or provocative transgression have become favored forms of originality and value.

So I think it is vital that we keep asking what really causes value and originality and also for whose benefit are those criteria being established. The answers to these questions help us to reflect on how we understand ambiguous relationships between creativity and dyslexia, stressing the importance of having an appropriate model of imagination for a responsible creative education.

Richard Kearney has argued for a three part model of imagination. He rethinks what's usually called adaption as the testimonial function for imagination and he rethinks innovation as its Utopian function, but critically he then adds what he calls the empathetic function of imagination – that function which opens us up to empathise with other peoples' difference and hopefully helps stop schoolboys finding creative ways of stealing hard-earned cigarettes from school cleaners through understanding another's point of view. It is this empathetic imagination which informs Geraldine Finn's statement about categories and which gives ethical orientation to the simple adaptive innovative model of creativity.

I believe passionately that for creativity to be genuinely original and valuable it needs to be in touch with each of these three different aspects of imagination. I would end by speculating that given the design mind's tendency to be a more intuitive, pattern searching and holistic form of thinking, it might relish Kearney's non binary, less linear, model of imagination. If this is the case it suggests that this educational approach which would be of benefit to design minds should also be used to develop the imaginative ability of all those in all disciplines, not just those currently designated as creative. If that were to happen there would be no such thing as dyslexia, only a rich variety and diversity of ways of thinking about the world.

To conclude Iain showed slides from Art Works, a collection edited by Iain Biggs, made with colleagues from the Arts Dyslexia Trust and designed and printed by Jonathon Ward and a team of staff at the print centre of the University of the West of England.

Prints in the book were made by established professionals and by recent art Graduates, many of whom are dyslexic, to remind us of richness and diversity of skills and concerns of the people who make them. These included a drawing by John Gunter, theatre designer which demonstrated using imaginative visualisation to aid the practical construction of artifacts; work by Sally Morgan, a key figure in developing community and public art; a print by Robert Rauschenberg, internationally renown painter who is also dyslexic; installation by Daphne Wright, a sculptor and installation artist who combines traditional materials with intrusions such as sound, and is interested in issues of feminism and identity; Work by Anthony Gormley, the 1994 Turner prize winner who has been credited with revitalising the use of the human figure in contemporary sculpture; a drawing by Lord Richard Rogers, an exemplary dyslexic architect who has stressed the importance of the relationships between architecture, the environment and society and who, like Gunter, uses his energized drawing as a practical tool; Ruth Solomon whose work reflects responses to music and Hilary Wells, MA RCA, who now deals with metaphors for complex and apparently disconnected states of mind. Which, as Iain said, was a good place to end.

References

Biggs, I (ed) (1998) *Art Works,* Artists' limited edition book (50) with 20 artists' prints (Arts Dyslexia Trust).

Finn, G (1996) Why *Althusser Killed His Wife: Essays on Discourse and Violence* (New Jersey: Humanities Press).

Kearney, R (2002) *Strangers, Gods and Monsters: Interpreting Otherness* (London & New York: Routledge).

Steffert, B (1999) *Visual-spatial Ability and Dyslexia* (London: Central Saint Martin's School of Art).

All Our Futures: Creativity, Culture and Education (1999) Report written by the National Advisory Committee on Creative and Cultural Education, (Report to: the Secretary of State for Education and Employment, the Secretary of State for Culture, Media and Sport).

The Visual Arts, Visual and Sculptural Communication

Andrew Henon

During the 'Cascade' conference the arts were represented in a number of ways. Together with performance pieces by Ketaki Kushari Dyson with her play 'Night's Sunlight' and Duncan McLeod's Music installation, there was an exhibition of invited artists and the installation of a number of site and event specific works presented at key venues during the conference.

This paper focuses on the works installed at the key venues at the conference and the works by the same artists included in the exhibition. It relates to the importance of a visual and experiential form of communication, the content and conceptual elements of the pieces the context and connections with issues covered in the conference. It looks at the importance of a visual language and how we respond with an inner dialogue on encountering visual art. These works provided a number of different functions during the event. They were opportunities for artists to contribute towards the conference with a presence other than verbal or text based communication. The artworks themselves provided visual and experiential orientation points for delegates at the conference as well as additional connected conversation pieces.

The artworks that are reviewed and described here can't be explained, analysed or described fully in text form. We live in a complex social culture and visual artwork produced by artists in our culture has to be viewed in that context. It is the collective experience of artists, viewers and the work itself that creates the dialogue. The dialogue is present during the production of the work; this becomes integral to the work as it precedes to completion and it remains once the work is finished. The dialogue is then continued as the work interfaces with another viewer. It is an immediate dialogue that builds on encountering the work itself. In many cases the dialogue is multi facetted, and begins at many points of access. Access can be through the materials in the first instance for example a touch, the tactile material qualities that can connect immediately with memory. Our lived experience may also produce an immediate interaction and reaction in some way with the work. The intensity of the interaction will depend on our own individual perceptions and lived experience.

There is however a deeper level of communication that at times is so intense that it becomes almost universal. It is this level of communication that many visual artists strive towards attaining. It is the direct universal visual and experiential language of communication that text can't fully attain. That is not to say that text is not a strong medium of communication and that the written word can't create a powerful response and the dialogue be of equal intensity on the imagination. It is more that this point of access is not as immediate or as direct. Even in this attempt to put the essence of a visual language into words it is rightly beyond me.

With the included images I ask you the reader to look at them first before reading my interpretation. The reader's interpretation may be different from mine and is of equal validity.

Karen Browning

Karen Browning installed an artwork entitled 'Cascade Wall' (fig 1, 1a, 1b) see left.

This particular part of the University has a ribbed concrete wall opposite the main lecture hall used during Cascade. It is a wall that although many thousands of people pass by year in year out, it is neither considered important, beautiful or interesting. However Karen painted the entrenched back surface of the ribs with Clear Ultra Violet reactive paint leaving an oval area of unpainted surface. The piece was then lit with an Ultra Violet Light source.

It relates to exposing that which already exists in literally a different light. In daylight the shape is invisible yet under certain conditions something is revealed, the revelation is still an area of unpainted concrete however we now see this area as significant being delineated and formed by the painted strips. The wall itself is a barrier yet we begin to perceive that there is an opening an area that although not illuminated itself becomes evident because it's surroundings have been.

There is also an element of public interaction with the piece that is experiential as seen in the photograph, on close interaction with the piece the viewer interferes with the image, a shadow is cast on the wall and a silhouette appears. Not only does the viewer experience a change in the installation on a personal level but other viewers also experience another element of the installation. A light reactive painted concrete wall becomes an experiential event. This is in stark contrast to the use of the space on a daily basis and uses the ordinary in an extraordinary way.

Jeff Body

Jeff Body installed an artwork entitled 'World Herd' and exhibited 'New Fossils.com'

'World Herd' was produced in response to the BSE and Foot & Mouth Crisis experienced in the year prior to the Cascade conference. It was installed in the foyer of the conference reception and meeting area of workshop venues. The piece was produced in reconstructed stone moulded from a set of Water Buffalo Horns. World Herd is an installation of progressively smaller stone horns stacked on top of each other into a conical interlocked piece.

World Herd both relates to issues current at the time and to larger issues of sustainability and timeless history. The piece is communicating on a number of levels as a memorial and as a statement of loss a sense of countless ageless disaster. The viewer is invited to encounter this piece both as a visual and tactile experience. With the stone there is a sense of fossilisation, a turning to stone. In isolation the piece resonates with the issues of mortality, the mortality of our natural world, our own mortality and mass consumer culture. It also refers to the consumer culture of our time, apparently bereft of moral humanity, consumption at any cost, mass production applied to the food chain and the industrialisation of animal welfare. The piece speaks to us of mass animal genocide and forces us to confront our inner emotions and feelings. At the height of the foot and mouth crisis it became evident that the systems employed in the industrialisation of animal agriculture, the structures and processes in place had failed, localised issues could not be contained, the cull spread rapidly to a national and international level.

We have also been subjected to a conveyor belt educational system and to the industrial processing of individuals. This piece offers us the opportunity to pause and reflect on the larger cultural issues we face.

New Fossils.com was exhibited in the library main exhibition. It is a piece that brings issues of access to the front of our consciousness. The computer age is one in which the most access is open to those that can afford it financially and or are technologically informed. The advances in computer science and the access to new technologies have still to reach a significant number of our population. We tend to forget as we upgrade our machines to broadband or increase our memory capacity and install the latest software that many people have never used a PC. The moulded computer mice, in resin held in stone, are as accessible and usable as they are to many people. The piece also relates to the mortality of this technology, again driven by a consumer culture, a choice of style or colour does not make it immortal. It may be that in the future the fossilised remains of computers will be discovered as unusable now as they may be in the future. When our e-mail crashes do our lives still continue? How important have our PC's become? New Fossils.com provides us with a salient reminder to all of us who have embraced the new technology into our lives that there are still many who have not.

Andrew Henon
Andrew Henon installed an artwork entitled 'Blocks'

The piece was installed on the Wall of the main lecture theatre used during the conference. It is a sculptural relief that uses children's primary painted wooden building blocks and a back lit computer circuit board, within a widow frame. The primary colours used to identify components used on the circuit board echo the primary colours of the blocks. As we access our own memories of playing with building blocks either as children or as parents we are prevented from accessing the memory stored in the circuit board. The visual message communicates the relationship between the two synthetic building elements both the blocks and the circuit are toys, what we build in our own imagination is based on our memories, connections that we may be consciously unaware of.

The building blocks of both elements adhere to strict guidelines and rules of use, their shape and form and the possible relationships between them define the parameters of use. Both elements are not flexible they require the employment of a sequential method in order to create something new. Both elements combine in a piece that itself becomes a 'block'; the viewer can neither play with the building blocks nor use the computer circuit. The viewer is however prompted to access their own memory or wonder at the complexity of the structures. Through the exposure of the circuit, something that is not usually visible, the relationship between the building blocks can clearly be seen. Often the frustration with computer use is that in order to use them we have to conform to a strict sequential method. The same as when a child meets the restrictions of using the blocks, a tower is fun to knock over but can be frustrating to build.

Andrew Henon Exhibited two paintings in the Cascade Exhibition, entitled 'Report' and 'New Growth'

Report seen here is very dark piece and was produced in response to a revisiting of previous school reports and school experiences. The surface is pitted and ripped the ink smudged and blurred. The dark horizontal vertical grey oppressive form confines the centre of the painting. The centre painting is confined further by the use of red and dark black out towards and including the frame. The inference is that however much the interior of the painting changes it will always be constrained by the black and red. In much the same way as whatever is written in blue ink the red pen will always contain it. Small areas of light appear these are still held by the oppressive overriding dark red and are produced by the process of scraping in to the work or bleeding out along the frame.

The piece has been produced in a violent process and represents this process to the viewer; a lot of energy has been exhausted in the making of the image. The materials have been degraded, moulded and contorted on the surface. The frame of the painting is an integral part of it and painting is a tactile and visual response to reports and the memory of school.

New Growth was a single painting from a series of nine of the same name. The piece portrays the fragility and strength of organic growth. The complexity made from simplicity and the highly complex forms in nature. It is a visual feast of movement and organic growth, layers and depth.

The full set of nine works, were produced with the concept of change in mind each work develops and changes overtime. Some of these works were produced on paper impregnated with carbon the pigment used will react over a period of time and begin a process of degradation. Some of the works contain fluorescent pigment becoming more vibrant under different conditions.

Change is an important part of this body of work and in terms of a visual language emphasizes the possibilities of an ongoing form of communication, one that is not static.

The Cascade conference offered Karen Browning, Jeff Body and myself the opportunity to make a contribution from a position outside of the established academic institutional environment. As I mentioned in the introduction direct contact with visual art can't be fully expressed in text form. Only contact with the work, that encompasses the emotional aspects, the immediate time and place of encounter and the individual responses, the consequent dialogues developed at the time, together with the individual circumstances, awareness and current issues at the time of the encounter communicates effectively between the artwork and the viewer.

During the Cascade conference there were many contributions from the visual arts. Of the artists exhibiting in the exhibition Alan Rayner, Iain Biggs and Mike Juggins have contributed papers that refer to their own works and practice. John Harlow stoneware potter and then Director of Bath University Computing Services and Alan Rayner both amply demonstrated interdisciplinary ability. I have not referred to these works in this paper other than to say that I have the greatest respect for their work and the contribution that they have made both in the field of dyslexia, science, education and the visual arts.

Concluding comments and How can we enhance the flow of values that carry hope for the future of humanity?   Part 2.

This conclusion continues the edited transcript of the conclusion to the conference presented by Jack Whitehead, and attempts to identify some essential aspects for consideration in developing creativity across science, art, dyslexia, education.

One theme is that of subjectivity/objectivity, the need for the inclusion of the person in academia and the questioning of the exclusion of the "I" in so-called objective academic research.

Jack Whitehead described how in America they found the kind of question with an "I" in the content was very difficult to acknowledge that it was or could ever be an academic enquiry, Jack described how his own practice in living educational theory gives him the feeling that "what I'm trying to do in relation to my own self studies in practice relate across art, science, dyslexia and education". Jack explained in "How can I help you?" the 'I' is central even though the 'you' is crucial to the enquiry. Jack referred to Alan Rayner's (4) work in seeking "pleasurable engagement with living space" and invited the audience to share for a few moments what had been of value to them in the conference. Jack then stopped a hubbub of discussion with the words, "I have a feeling you could continue all afternoon." He acknowledged having the sense of being invited in to do something and the tension he experiences when breaking in to genuine dialogue between others for a purpose. He described the educational value of sharing what has been of value in the conference with others. "I just want to get a sense of how we can move from that quality where you are engaged with another person saying what really does matter to you, what is important into the group as a whole. That process of inclusion is really important in terms of talking about what this conference has been about and how to take it forward. If you are feeling slightly critical, you may have more the feeling that this is a flash of inspiration that like a flare can only blossom once and not come up again. I am not convinced, yet."

This process of inclusion requires safe space, a landscape free from ownership, neutral and accepting. The flares could, as in the oil fields, have gone underground – to pop up elsewhere. They could be easily extinguished, or the flame could burn in perpetuity as in the Olympic model.

Another common theme across the disciplines is that of sustainability. Whether the process and the time needed to make connections, form links and understand and respect different ways of working can be secured in an academia which is becoming increasingly product driven. You, the reader will realise that it is now six years on from the proceedings of this conference, and that it took place before the so-called 9/11 events. Was this event a brief flare? At times it has felt that it might have been. Many times I have thought that the ensuing global events tended to wipe out the value of all we had achieved in pulling Cascade together. As Jack said, the essential life affirming energy that we had experienced at Cascade needs to be celebrated collaboratively, but in the face of all we have seen during the ensuing years it has sometimes seemed like an impossible task.

Nevertheless not only have many of the participants of the conference formed networks, and stayed in touch with the other and developed new work, the call for more information about the proceedings continues slowly to grow. As Professor Gosling describes, we need dyslexic people, his own work with non exploding mine fields may prove to be one of the most life enhancing defence developments of the 21st century.

A theme that was repeatedly referred to is exclusion, the pain and the nature of exclusion. This centers on the lack of understanding and the resulting derogatory reaction from those who Will Gosling refers to as modal thinkers, "I could see it in their eyes". There is also something around language and the subtlety of the issues presented which makes them uncomfortable, sometimes non-verbal and therefore easier for non dyslexic people to ignore or avoid. This is common with other diversity issues. Ketaki Kushari Dyson spoke about this sense of exclusion and pain the performers of 'Night's Sunlight', a play whose content is intrinsic to widening participation debates, had experienced. Ketaki movingly expressed the difficulties and frustrations this presented. Jack responded that initially he had expected that Mo's introductory comparison of 'Night's Sunlight' with Ibsen was likely to be hyperbole, however he and Alan Rayner felt it was one of the most powerful dramatic experiences they had ever experienced, "It was profoundly moving – a sense of affirmation that really did connect with the audience – values that were so powerful and relate undoubtedly with creativity and the values of the conference". Margarida Dolan added that the play ends with the woman saying she still has something to say, and in the context of creativity this is profoundly moving, "We still have something to say".

Alan McLean said he gained a sense of empowerment, had enjoyed talking to other dyslexics and that he would actually promote dyslexia more as an issue within disability culture. Ann Brigden celebrated people doing things that can be affirmed by others, paintings produced by scientists and academics, who may have put themselves out on a limb by being courageous enough to be open about their own dyslexia, made her feel that the academic ivory tower was actually beginning to shake. She said, "too often we feel we are a minority within a somewhat suffocating culture in education. Imagination, embracing creativity, play and playing with ideas are part of the learning process." This element of celebration and joy was important to identify as a different quality which comes from the uncertain interdisciplinary process.

Will Gosling movingly expressed his concerns that while the conference and he himself had indulged in what he termed "dyslexia triumphalism", which needed to be done, he reminded us of Diane Little's description of the characteristics of dyslexia are both "the man rattling his tin cup across the bars of cell and the man going to receive his Nobel Prize". Will remained worried about the dyslexia who "is not very gifted, who cannot rise above the circumstances of the society and education in which he finds himself" and said that this person "had been haunting him throughout the conference."

Jane Graves believes that everybody has talent. She reminded us that we are in a hierarchical system which continues historically to be about exclusion and failure. "Criminals are hugely creative, but not in ways that we can appreciate very much. It is difficult for us to try and change a system imposed on us which is not really sympathetic to the idea of being an inclusive culture".

Jack concluded that in living educational theory everybody will need to address the power relations associated with legitimizing embodied knowledge and to explain what they are learning as they seek to live their values more fully in their practice (5). He pointed out that this sense of the political is so important in terms of enhancing the flow of values that carry hope for the future of humanity. Referring to Basil Bernstein's last book (6) where he talks about the trick of the mythology that is played out on us. "The trick is trying to believe you are creating within schools something that is quite separate from power and control, and not part of the control mechanisms of a wider society. We need to see the connections. What Will is saying about the knowledge and the way we need to transform it is part of the process. Each living educational thesis has had to address issues of power and control and not allow it to be distorted by the academy".

These power relations are very evident across the disciplines, with science appearing at first to hold sway over art and education. It becomes clear working with scientists that the best science is not the linear objective rationale we have been led to believe. Therefore there is another power base within education and teaching and learning that needs to be challenged. One common theme is the fear – for artists approaching science, for scientists approaching art, for dyslexic people approaching an education system that denies and derides their way of working, and for those in education faced with the need for change.

It becomes clearer that the dialogue that interdisciplinary and diverse work engages us in can be uncomfortable yet touches on some essential elements for human survival. We have much we can learn from this, and there is some urgency in the need for these issues to be addressed within academia. To conclude I repeat Jack's words, "It seems to me if we're going to have some influence in the world we've got to learn how to celebrate that life affirming energy collaboratively" and express the hope that this collection goes some way to achieving this aim.

References

Adler-Collins, J. (2004) Living Action Research. See http://www.living-action-research.net/

Adler-Collins, J. (2000) *A Scholarship of Enquiry'*. MA Dissertation, University of Bath. Retrieved 4 July 2004 from http://www.actionresearch.net/jekan.shtml

Boyer, E. (1990). *Scholarship reconsidered: Priorities of the professoriate.* The Carnegie Foundation for the Advancement of Teaching: Princeton University Press. Cambridge, B. (1999)

Rayner, A. (2004) *Essays and Talks on Inclusionality.* Retrieved 4 July 2004 from http://www.bath.ac.uk/~bssadmr/inclusionality/

Whitehead, J. (2004) What counts as evidence in self-studies of teacher education practices? In Loughran, J. J., Hamilton, M. L., LaBoskey, V. K. & Russell, T. (2004) International Handbook of Self-study of Teaching and Teacher Education Practices. Dordrecht; Kluwer Academic Publishers.

Bernstein, B. (2000) Pedagogy, Symbolic Control and Identity. See . pp. xii-xxiv. Oxford; Rowman & Littlefield.

After word

As an artist who is dyslexic I have personally encountered the change in acceptance, a tangible growth in the understanding of the subject. The many contributors and participants at the cascade conference have undertaken much of the research in the field of dyslexia over many years. This work has played a great part in being responsible for the sea change in attitudes and the massive growth in awareness of the issues both in education and our culture.

I would like to thank all of the delegates at this conference on a personal level. It is due to your work and commitment to the field of dyslexia that the school experiences that I encountered due to my dyslexia will hopefully not be repeated for my children and many, many others. I personally now have a greater understanding of my own thinking and doing processes and am able to reflect on my own practice in a much more informed way. Thank you to all of you.

Andrew Henon

Biographies

Dr Iain Biggs is Reader in Visual Art Practice and Director of Studies, Supervised Research Degrees at the Bristol School of Art, Media and Design, University of the West England. He co-convenes LAND2, a national network of artists associated with Higher Education and concerned with radical approaches to the complexity of representing land and landscape (http://www.land2.uwe.ac.uk/). Trained as a painter and printmaker, he currently makes artist's books and related collaborative work, and writes. He has a particular interest in issues of memory, place and identity in relation to contemporary art and has published on this and on a range of contemporary artists.
Iain.Biggs@uwe.ac.uk

Ketaki Kushari Dyson, born in Calcutta in 1940 and educated at Calcutta and Oxford, is regarded as an outstanding Bengali writer of her generation. She has continued to write in Bengali though she has been part of the Indian Diaspora in Britain for well over three decades. Kidlington, near Oxford, has been her permanent home since 1969. She writes in several literary genres, including poetry, fiction, drama, translation, and research-based works. A noted translator, who translates between her two languages in both directions with equal fluency, she has translated Anglo-Saxon poetry into Bengali, Rabindranath Tagore's poetry into English (Bloodaxe Books, 1991, Poetry Book Society Recommended Translation), and is currently translating the poetry of Buddhadeva Bose.

Professor William Gosling read physics under Sir George Thomson; A.R.C.S; BSc U of London; D.Sc. (Electronic Engineering) U of Bath. Degrees honoris causa from UMIST and Plymouth U. After graduating, he spent five years with the de Havilland Company then joined the Swansea University as a Lecturer, elected Professor of Electrical Engineering 1966. In 1974 he moved to the first Chair of Electronic Engineering at the newly founded University of Bath- now Professor emeritus. At the end of 1980 he was recruited by the Plessey Company, joining their Board as Group Technical Director and leaving them at the end of 1989 (Plessey was taken-over by GEC and Siemens).

First UK President Convention des Societes Des Electriciens de l'Europe Occidentale (EUREL), Fellow and past-President Institution of Electrical Engineers, Fellow Institute of Directors, Liveryman of the Worshipful Company of Scientific Instrument Makers, Freeman of the City of London, and Life Member of the Association of Old Crows. Has published fifty scientific papers and fourteen books, and has written for The Telegraph and The Guardian. Member of the Athenaeum, High-Church Anglican and married with two surviving children.

Jane Graves was a Lecturer in cultural studies at Central Saint Martin's College of Art and Design for nearly thirty years. She now works as a psychoanalytical psychotherapist. Marrying these two disparate fields she writes and publishes in the field of psychoanalysis and design. She is particularly interested in the nature of creativity in these areas. She first became interested in dyslexia about fifteen years ago after a bruising encounter with a student who had the courage to tell her she was getting things badly wrong. As a result she undertook a training as a specialist dyslexia tutor and set up a voluntary support system. In 1996 the London Institute agreed to set up a research programme to explore a possible relationship between dyslexia and visual-spatial ability. Even more important, the Institute agreed to train other established and respected academic staff to take on additional responsibilities as dyslexia support tutors.

Dr. Mary Haslum is Reader in Psychology and was Coordinator of Postgraduate Studies in Psychology at the University of the West of England. She is a Chartered Psychologist and an Associate Fellow of the British Psychological Society. Dr. Haslum's research interest in dyslexia began when as Principal Research Officer she was responsible for the 10-year follow-up of the 17,000 children of the British Berths National Cohort Study. Her work has focused on children with dyslexia, motor coordination difficulties, vision and hearing difficulties and children who are hospitalised in the first five years of life. She has also conducted nationwide surveys of screening for hearing and vision defects in children. Dr, Haslum now carries out research on dyslexia with students in Higher Education and is currently working on the provision of on-line assessment and learning support for students with study and learning difficulties.

Andrew Henon combines and integrates conceptual and creative thinking within socially engaged participatory arts practice. The work focuses on site and need based specifics, working in many different contexts with a diversity of groups and partners. This is an ongoing process towards the resolution of social, economic, geographical and environmental issues. Over a period of thirty years Andrew has integrated his practice as a lifestyle and life's work, undertaking studio and non-studio based practice, interventions, lead artist roles, enabling, facilitating roles and projects. Andrew is well known in the South West as an advocate and practitioner of social inclusion, economic, cultural and social development and collective and individual creativity. His work is an ongoing inquiry into the understanding of nature, human behaviour, connections, interactions, dynamics and underlying creativity.

Professor Margaret Herrington is Visiting Professor of Education, University of Wolverhampton and Special Lecturer in Continuing Education at the University of Nottingham. She undertook qualitative research culminating in the report Working with Dyslexic Students in Higher Education, Department for Education and Skills (2004) as part of the Learning and Skills Development Agency/National Institute of Adult and Continuing Education dyslexia research project 2003-04. She is the author of New Policies: Old Dilemmas (1995) RaPAL Journal 27, and Dyslexia: The Continuing Exploration, (2001) RaPAL Journal 46 among many others. Margaret continues to make a major contribution towards developing our understanding of the educational issues for dyslexia at every level.

Mike Juggins Is a dyslexic artist. I have spent many years developing my interest in the relationship between image, text and ideas. My study at the University of the West of England produced a dissertation titled dyslexics in a word based education system and led to a contextualised residency within an educational setting. I have exhibited and given lectures at a number of establishments nationally during the last eight years, forming an extensive network of contacts in the process, and developing understanding of dyslexia including film on Channel 4.

Morag Kiziewicz is Learning Support Manager at the University of Bath. http://www.bath.ac.uk/learningsupport . Her first career was in environmental design, she then became course director in spatial design at the Arts Institute, Bournemouth prior to joining the University of Bath, a role that included the brief to develop access for dyslexia in Higher Education in the South west region. The WEBB Dyslexia Project, 1997 - 2000, included a comparative study on identification and intervention for dyslexia, together with action on institution issues. www.bath.ac.uk/learningsupport/webb/dyslexia.htm . The findings were disseminated during the Cascade event. Mo's research interests include visual spatial ability applied across all disciplines, developing access to Higher Education for diversity and connections with creativity, cognition and dyslexia. In Teaching and Learning she is exploring holistic approaches to the accessible curriculum, including virtual learning environments and alternative approaches to assessment and inclusive education.

Professor Tim Miles was appointed Professor of Psychology at the University of Wales, Bangor in 1963. He retired in 1987 and is now Professor Emeritus. His main research interest has been developmental dyslexia. He and his wife, Elaine, have lectured on the subject in many different parts of the world- in the USA, in Australia and New Zealand, and on the continent of Europe. In 1996 they were joint recipients of the International Dyslexia Association Award for International Leadership, and in 2001 they jointly received the Marion Welchman award for lifelong services to dyslexia.

Tim is editor of Dyslexia: An International Journal of Research and Practice, published by John Wiley & Sobs. He has also published books on behaviorism and on the philosophy of religion. He captained Oxford University at lawn tennis and played in the championships at Wimbledon in 1946 and 1948. He is an amateur cellist and keen croquet player.

Ian Padgett was a director of studies for research degrees at the London Institute's Central Saint Martins College of Art and Design. His personal research interests, emanate from consideration of the cognitive and methodological processes involved in the realisation of creative solutions or problematics of design, which were encountered both as a designer in the textile and fashion industry and as a postgraduate teacher. He was involved in the organisation of the conferences "Artsdyslex One" (at the Art Workers Guild London) and "Genius in the Genes" (at Oxford University Green College). He edited the publication "Visual Spatial Ability and Dyslexia" which reported upon the research project conducted at Central Saint Martins undertaken by Dr Beverly Steffert. In his capacity as joint Vice-Chairman of the Arts Dyslexia Trust he continues to be actively involved in the promotion of visual spatial ability as an "individual cognitive style".

Dr David Pollak first worked with dyslexic learners as a teacher in 1974. He has supported students of all ages from year two to adult. Since 1995 he has been working in higher education learning support, and is also currently course leader of the MA in Dyslexia Studies at De Montfort University. David's PhD focused on the learning life histories of undergraduates who are dyslexic. His other interests include counselling and classical singing.

Dr Alan D. M. Rayner was born on 26/07/50, and is a Reader in the Department of Biology and Biochemistry at the University of Bath. He was the President of the British Mycological Society in 1998. He has published over 125 scientific articles and six books, including "Degrees of freedom: Living in Dynamic boundaries" (Imperial College Press, 1997). His wide interests range from sub-cellular to ecosystem-level scales of biological organization and he is a keen naturalist with knowledge of plant, animal and fungal ecology, diversity and classification. He is currently exploring new ways of understanding the dynamic relationships between genes and environment, based on the effects of physical and chemical feedback and oxidative stress at living systems boundaries. He is a founder of "Bio*Art", an art form which expresses and draws inspiration from the dynamic boundaries of living systems.

Dr Guy Saunders currently teaching social psychology at the University of The West of England, Bristol. Studied Fine Art (Sculpture) at St Martin's School of Art in 1970s. After a miscellany of job, took degree in Psychology at Middlesex, then Phd at Bath (finished in 1999). Research focussed on accounts of the experience of solitary confinement given by former hostages and political prisoners as a way of investigating the use, enactment and experience of imagination.

Dr Jack Whitehead has worked as a Lecturer in Education at the University of Bath since 1973. His research into the nature of educative relations, influence and theory has focused on the use of embodied values as living standards of educational practice and judgment. The homepage actionresearch.net contains many of his publications including recent keynotes to conferences in Greece, Ireland and Canada. The living theory theses of his research students are providing much needed support for researchers who are engaging in first person enquiries of the kind, How do I live my values more fully in my practice? The living standards of practice and judgment he embodies in his own educational practice and research include originality of mind and critical judgment. Jack is a former President of the British Educational Research Association, a visiting professor at Brock University in Ontario and a Distinguished Scholar in Resident of Westminster College, Utah.